Critical Guides to French Texts

Critical Guides to French Texts

EDITED BY ROGER LITTLE, WOLFGANG VAN EMDEN,
DAVID WILLIAMS

The Romance of the Rose

Sarah Kay

Girton College
Cambridge

Grant & Cutler Ltd
1995

DEPÓSITO LEGAL: V. 4.284 - 1995

Printed in Spain by
Artes Gráficas Soler, S. A. - La Olivereta, 28 - 46018 Valencia
for
GRANT & CUTLER LTD
55-57 GREAT MARLBOROUGH STREET, LONDON W1V 2AY

Contents

Preface

This study refers to the edition of the *Romance of the Rose* by Daniel Poirion (*3*)*, a one-volume paperback which is cheap, portable, and still easily obtainable at the time of writing. It is based on a different manuscript from the edition by Felix Lecoy (*2*): *Z* (BN fr. 25523) as opposed to *H* (BN fr. 1573). On occasion, Poirion includes lines from *H* where there is an omission in *Z*. Lecoy's is the next most user-friendly edition of the romance, and I give line references to it in square brackets following those from Poirion, in cases where they differ. Poirion's edition has the same line numbering as the earlier edition by Ernest Langlois (*1*). Langlois's edition is based on the collation of numerous MSS and attempts a reconstitution of the text's original dialect. Readers who have access to it can thus refer to it using the line references I provide, although they will find differences of detail, especially of orthography. The Langlois edition forms the basis of the most reliable English-language translation of the romance, that by Charles Dahlberg (*4*). Dahlberg provides sufficient line references to key his translation into the Old French text, and so his translation may also be used in conjunction with Poirion's. A further translation, based on Lecoy, was published in 1994 by Frances Horgan (*5*). The translations in this study are my own.

I should like to thank Leslie Brook, James Simpson, and especially Wolfgang van Emden, for their helpful comments on my typescript. My notional reader was Paula Leverage, who as an undergraduate disliked the *Romance of the Rose*. This book records my imaginary efforts to persuade her of its merits, and it is to her that I dedicate it.

---

* Italicised numerals in parentheses followed, where appropriate, by a page number refer to the numbered items in the bibliography at the end of this volume.

1. Text and Continuation

The *Romance of the Rose*, which was the most widely read, imitated, admired and debated work of the French Middle Ages, owed its success – its survival even – to a characteristically medieval literary practice: that of continuation. Many medieval works prompted *remanieurs* to extend or expand them; most surviving *chansons de geste* have been reworked in this way, for example, while lyric poems have sprouted additional stanzas, and romances (most notably Chrétien's *Conte del graal*) have inspired sequels. In the case of the *Romance of the Rose* the continuation is four times as long as the text it is allegedly composed to complete, and attracted a far wider readership. That, at least, is the picture which emerges from the surviving manuscripts. Of over two hundred and fifty, only one contains a text with no trace of this continuation; it has a short (76-line) ending composed by an unknown author. All the remainder combine the original text by Guillaume de Lorris with the continuation which made it famous and which names its author Jean de Meun. Another *remanieur*, Gui de Mori, claims to have drafted his own continuation before he encountered Jean's and accommodated his own to it (*36*, p.40). The original *Rose*, apparently incomplete, survives because it stirred the critical imagination of medieval readers. The variations between different families of manuscripts show that this process of critical reading and adaptation went on even after the *Rose* had been 'completed' by Jean de Meun (*38, passim*).

Jean was a poet and an intellectual with a flair for popularising learned material, and a brilliant vein of humour. His other known works, apart from a *Testament* and *Codicile* of uncertain attribution, are all translations from Latin, marked by a vigorous and engaging style (*19*, pp.103-16). He translated Vegetius's *De Re Militari*, and nearer the time of his death in 1305,

the *De Consolatione Philosophiae* or *Consolation of Philosophy* by
the fifth-century philosopher Boethius (*13*, p.86), familiarity with
which is evident throughout his continuation of the *Rose*. (Two
other translations, of Giraldus Cambrensis and Aelred of Rivaulx,
have not survived.) But Jean's translation of Abelard's autobiography, and of his correspondence with Heloise, although little
quoted in the *Rose* (see 8759-824 [8729-94], of which 8817-24
[8787-94] closely follow Letter II), illumines it just as much as does
the often-cited *Consolation* (see for instance 5037 [5007], 6299
[6269]). Abelard's passionate and and perilous encounter with
sexuality, and the ensuing confrontations between sex and secular
power, sex and the clerical life, and later (since Heloise judged it in
his interests that they should not marry) between sex and marriage,
place his autobiography on a knife-edge between sensuality and
social or spiritual norms. Later in the *History*, when Abelard's
theological work is condemned, conflict flares up once more as
intellect is opposed to orthodoxy, reason to repression. These
clashes led to Abelard's castration, both physically and, when his
book was destroyed, symbolically. Abelard's narrative and letters,
and the letters ascribed to Heloise, thus confront in an early twelfth-
century context the issues which Jean was to address in the *Rose*;
his continuation is constantly alert to contradictions between the
sexual, intellectual, social and theological claims on the individual,
and to the discourses in which these claims are lodged. Indeed, he
probably composed his continuation in the 1270s, and before 1278:
in the context, that is, of the condemnation, by the bishop of Paris in
1277, of the 'pagan' content of Arts courses at the University of
Paris (*59*, pp.12-21 and *43*, *passim*), at a time when scandal,
libertinism and repression were in the air.

     Without Jean de Meun, we should not know the identity of the
author of the original *Rose*, whom Jean names as Guillaume de
Lorris, further asserting that he died some forty years before Jean
wrote. This places the date of the first part of the *Rose* around 1235,
though there is some disagreement over this (see most recently *36*,
p.213 fn.). Guillaume's *Rose* is not only shorter, it is more elegant,
decorous, controlled, and easier to read than its incendiary but

seemingly endlessly ramifying 'ending'. Manuscripts of it seem to have circulated before the addition of Jean's continuation turned it into a *succès de scandale*. Although Guillaume's narrative apparently breaks off in mid-lament, at least one modern scholar has argued that it is complete (*36*, pp.105-85). It is possible, then, to study Guillaume de Lorris's *Rose* as a text in its own right.

But Jean did more than devise an end for Guillaume's narrative. He also read his text attentively, seriously as well as irreverently. In the passage where he names the two authors of the poem he clearly has Guillaume's text open before him, quoting the last lines of it together with the opening lines of his continuation (see Chapter 3, pp.40-41). Towards the end of the *Rose*, the figure of Genius comments closely on Guillaume's text (see Chapter 5, pp.84-87). Continuation is supplementation: the continuator both acknowledges the qualities of his model, and sets out to 'improve' it, thus implying it also has shortcomings. Jean's *Rose* quotes, criticises, parodies and engages in many other ways with its source. In some ways, his continuation is less an expansion than an explosion of the original *Rose*. Although it is possible to read the work of Guillaume de Lorris on its own, I think therefore that it is preferable to read it in its continued form. Jean de Meun (henceforth JdM) was an extraordinary reader – not just of Guillaume de Lorris (GdL) – and it is in acknowledgement of his critical acumen that this study of the *Romance of the Rose* will proceed.

2. Allegory and Irony

Most early medieval French texts exhibit a tension between two different notions of the real. There is a sensory, tangible, here-and-now reality, but there is also a reality of a different order, of abstract values such as love, knighthood, nature. In the romances of Chrétien, for instance, there are 'realistic' descriptions of a textile workshop (*Yvain*) or knighting ceremonies (*Conte del graal*), of court ceremonial, clothing, and church services. Much of the so-called *merveilleux* of these romances jars with this 'realism' of the observable daily round; but it suggests another realm of *realia* of a less tangible kind. The sparrowhawk episode in *Erec* is set up by a series of 'unrealistic' events, but it invokes abstract realities such as love, adventure, individuality, and social responsibility. Most critical writings on Chrétien are concerned with extrapolating the complexities of these abstract meanings, asking whether they are primarily emotional, ethical, sociopolitical (concerned with knighthood or monarchy, for example), or intellectual (are the romances a debating-ground of philosophical issues?). Marie de France's *Lais* owe much of their charm to the equivocation between these two levels which results from her use of key emblems, 'real' in themselves, yet also gesturing towards an abstract reality of a different kind.

This movement of the medieval text between two notions of the real is a kind of 'allegory', in that the reader (or listener) is invited to find abstract (or spiritual) meanings alongside the more familiar meanings of mundane reality. The definition of allegory in Quintilian's *Institutionis oratoria* (widely known in the Middle Ages) is that allegory involves saying one thing and meaning another: 'aliud verbis, aliud sensu ostendit' (Book VIII.vi). It demands a reading beyond the literal details of a text, in order to construct a more distant level of meaning that is less obviously 'there'. Allegory, then, involves indirectness on the part of the text and an effort of interpretation on the part of its readers, whose ultimate understanding of it may differ markedly from their initial one. This construal of ulterior meaning, or allegoresis, can be performed only by an élite of clever, literate readers (see e.g. *71*, pp.91, 257), since the abstract significance is assumed to be in some way 'hidden' behind the literal one. The figure of Raison in JdM's continuation invokes this esoteric, learned tradition:

> Si dist l'en bien en nos escoles
> maintes choses par paraboles
> qui mout sont beles a entendre.
> Si ne doit l'en mie tout prendre
> a la lettre, quanque l'en ot.
> [...]
> Et qui bien entendroit la lettre,
> le sens verroit en l'escriture
> qui esclarsist la chose oscure.
> La verité dedens repote
> seroit clere, s'ele ert espote;
> bien l'entendras se bien repetes
> les integumens as poetes.
> La verras une grant partie
> des secrés de philosofie...*
>
> (7153-57, 7162-70 [7123-57, 7132-40])

'Integument' is the covering of art which poets cast over the 'kernel' of truth (*78*, pp.36-48).

There is, however, also a tradition of didactic writing in the Middle Ages that uses allegory in a different spirit: as a device not for hiding meanings but for making the invisible visible, and for

---

* 'And indeed in our schools many things are said in parables pleasing to the ear. But you mustn't take literally everything you hear. [...] To under-stand the letter of the text aright is to see the meaning of the writing, as it lights up that which is obscure. The truth hidden within would become clear if it were expounded. You will understand this if you review the "integuments" of the poets. There you will find most of the secrets of philosophy...'

rendering accessible the abstruse. When moralising poets present passions or ideas as people, and experiences as configurations of such people in a determinate space (such as a castle under siege, or a garden), they are making explicit to their readers ideas which they might otherwise find elevated or obscure. This explicitness of allegory has led to unfavourable comparison with the greater suggestiveness of symbolism (*39*, pp.110 ff.). In Chrétien, abstract meanings may be inferred from a literal narrative about individuals, but in explicitly didactic writing the levels of meaning are reversed: the 'abstract' level provides the stuff of 'character' and 'plot', whilst the inferred meaning relates to possible real-world events. Thus, to take as an example Raison's address to the dreamer, the actual scene presents the interaction of two characters, one of whom, Reason, lives in a tower, but the inferred meaning is that an individual is subject to the misgivings prompted by the 'higher' reflections of rationality.

The *Rose* is generally thought of as an allegory. Its réaders are under constant pressure to interpret, to look for 'hidden' meanings, and to ask themselves what kinds of reality are envisaged. 'Difficulty' is thereby brought into play. On the other hand, the text calls attention to a further level of meaning in a particularly explicit way, by the device of personification, and by declarations of didactic intent. Its technique is thus teasing and intriguing: it insists both that the poem's meaning is elusive, and that it is obvious. I look first at the gestures towards 'difficulty' and then at those towards 'explicitness'. The thread of the argument throughout is that JdM exercises his wit at the expense of his predecessor, and specifically, that he develops the potentially ironic elements in GdL's poem. Rather than reaping the two meanings, literal and figurative, of allegory, the reader is left in doubt about the possibility of assigning any determinate meaning at all, and finds the text's 'explicitness' as resistant to interpretation as its cultivated opacity.

(i) The dream

GdL's *Rose* starts as a dream. The prologue affirms, following Macrobius, a fourth-century author cited in line 7, that dreams

contain in covert form meanings which will later become apparent
(18-20). The promise to explicate this hidden meaning is reiterated
on several occasions, most clearly in this passage:

> des or le [= le roman] fet bon escouter,
> s'il est qui le sache conter,
> car la matire en est novelle
> et la fin du songe est mout belle.
> Qui du songe la fin orra,
> je vous di bien que il porra
> des jeus d'Amors assés aprendre,
> par quoi il vueille bien entendre
> [que je die et que j'encomance
> dou songe la senefiance.] H.
> La verité qui est couverte
> vous sera lores descouverte
> quant espondre m'orrés le songe,
> car il n'i a mot de mençonge.* (2063-76 [2061-74])

If the dream is no lie, however, the promise is; perhaps because, as
Hult suggests, the dream constructs a story of seduction which it
would be impolitic in a courtly aspirant to complete. JdM has no
such scruples. As he hastens the seducer along a path of increasing
cynicism, he breaks off for a moment to anticipate objections, using
words that certainly echo, and probably parody, the passage just
quoted:

> Notés ce que ci vois disant,
> d'amors avrés art souffisant.
> Et se vous y trovés rienz trouble
> qui vostre conscience trouble,

---

* 'From this point the romance is well worth listening to, if there is anyone
who can tell it, for its substance is new and the end of the dream very
beautiful. Anyone who hears the end of the dream will, I assure you, be
able to learn a great deal about the games of Love provided he pays heed
while I begin to tell the meaning of the dream. The truth which is hidden
will then be uncovered for you, when you hear me interpret the dream, for
it is entirely truthful.'

> quant le songe m'orrés espondre,
> bien savrés lors d'amors respondre,
> s'il est qui en sache opposer,
> quant le texte m'orrés gloser.*   (15143-50 [15113-20])

The expertise to be gained from the poem, he says, will be more
than enough to compensate for any qualms of conscience. But
although the end of the dream in his continuation is, in its way,
quite explicit (see pp.20-22), the dream is never 'glossed' in the
scholastic sense of having its difficulties explicated. Indeed, the one
dream in the poem which is explained (Croesus's, recounted by
Raison, 6501-622 [6471-592]) casts doubt on the value of
interpretation, since Croesus himself clings to his literal reading
that he will be elevated, and attended by gods: he rejects his
daughter's (correct) interpretation that this is an allegory of his
being hanged from a tree and buffeted by the weather, and so dies –
from his point of view – unexpectedly.

There is no dramatic unveiling of the truth of the poem's
principal dream. Instead JdM undermines belief in the existence of
such truth. The figure of Nature, who appears late on in the
continuation, denounces dreaming as one of many sources of human
illusion:

> ... qui, par grant devocion,
> en trop grant contemplacion,
> font aparoir en lor pensees
> les choses qu'ils ont porpensees,
> et les cuident tout proprement
> veoir defors apertement;
> et ce n'est fors trufle et mençonge,
> ausinc cum de l'omme qui songe,
> qui voit, ce cuide, en lor presences,

---

* 'Note what I am saying here, you will have sufficient skill in love. And if
you find anything turbid in what I say that troubles your conscience, later,
when you hear me expound the dream, you will be qualified to debate
about love, if you have an opponent who wishes to do so, once you hear me
gloss the text.'

les espirituex sustances
si cum fist Scipion jadis.
Et voit enfer et paradis
[...]
et baleries et karoles.
et ot vïeles et citoles
et flere espices odoreuses,
et goute choses savoreuses,
et gist entre les bras s'amie,
et toutevois n'i est il mie;
ou voit Jalousie venant
ung pestel a son col tenant,
qui provés ensemble les trueve
par Male Bouche qui contrueve
les choses ains que faites soient,
dont tuit amant par jour s'esmaient.
Car cil qui fins amans se clament
[...]
si songent les choses amees
que tant ont par jour reclamees;
ou songent de lor aversaires
qui lor font anuis et contraires.*

(18357-67, 18383-95, 18401-04
[18327-37, 18353-65, 18371-74])

---

* '...there are some who, through great piety, in an excess of contemplation, conjure up in their imagination the things they have reflected on and fancy that they really see them outside themselves, openly. And all this is nothing but lies and illusions, just as it is for the man who dreams and imagines that he can see spiritual essences as actuality, as Scipio did of old [this is a reference to Macrobius]. He sees hell and paradise [...] and dances of different kinds, and hears viols and citolas and smells fragrant spices and tastes delicious things and lies in the arms of his lady – which he certainly isn't doing – and sees Jalousie coming with a club on his shoulder and Malebouche inventing things before they've even been done, causing all lovers daily grief. For all who style themselves true lovers [...] dream of what they love, that they have desired all day, or else dream of the enemies who obstruct and torment them.'

What makes this passage particularly piquant is that it rehearses elements from the story of GdL's *Rose*, thus subverting his prologue and recategorising his dream not as 'truth' but as 'delusion', by means of a technique of narrative scattering or 'dissemination' (see 25) that will be examined in Chapter 4, pp.65-70. With this move, JdM shifts the poem from allegory towards irony, in that he admits doubt about the possibility of constructing any secure meanings, absent or not. (If Hult is right that GdL could never have finished his own dream, then his *Rose* is affected by irony also.)

(ii) Metaphor

This is the second major device for inviting (doubt about) interpretation. GdL's poem initiates a romance-like quest whose object is the rose. The exact nature of this object of desire has been much debated (is it a lady? her love? her virginity?). It is given an autobiographical resonance in the prologue where the poet claims to undertake his work for love of one:

> ... qui tant a de pris
> et tant est digne d'estre amee
> qu'el doit estre rose clamee.* (42-44)

But this resonance cannot be reduced to an identification of the rose of the dream with an individual woman, real or fictional. Instead, the rose remains a mysterious and eroticised object. Looking into the crystals in the pool of the Fontainne d'Amor, the dreamer first sees a multitude of roses, and then selects his favourite:

> entre ces boutons en eslui
> un si tres bel, qu'envers celui
> nus des autres riens ne prisé
> puisque je l'oi bien avisé;
> car une color l'enlumine
> qui est si vermeille et si fine
> con Nature la pot plus faire.

---

* '... who is so excellent, so worthy of love, that she is entitled to be called a rose.'

De foilles y ot quatre paire,
que Nature par grant mestire
i ot assises tire a tire;
la coe est droite comme jons
et par dessus siet li boutons
si qu'il ne cline ne ne pent.
L'odor de lui entor s'espent;
[...]
Quant je le senti si flairier,
je n'oi talent de repairier,
ains m'en apressai por lui prendre,
se g'i osasse la main tendre;
mes chardons agus et poignant
m'en aloient mout esloignant...*
(1655-68, 1671-76 [1651-66, 1669-74])

There are pointers here to ethical meanings (the straightness of the stem) and to social ones (the difficulty of access). The dreamer does indeed subsequently find the rose hard to approach, and is told to allow it to 'grow and improve' (2916 [2900]); and when it does so, it 'swells' whilst remaining closed around its seed (3357-70 [3339-52]). In fact the rose remains disconcertingly rose-like, and the dreamer's objective is to pick it (2902-04 [2886-88]), or kiss it (3386-94 [3368-76]); he is delighted by the gift of a leaf (2876-79 [2860-63]).

The rose thus faces the reader with the problem not only of what it might mean, but also of how metaphorical it is. It is placed in a garden setting which increases rather than reduces these

---

* 'Among those buds, I selected one so extremely beautiful that, in comparison with it, I had no concern for any of the others, once I had picked it out; for it glows with a colour as red and exquisite as Nature could make. There were four pairs of leaves that Nature, with great expertise, has set there, one after the other. Its stem is as straight as a reed, and the bud stands on it neither bowed nor hanging. The scent from it spread all around; [...] When I smelt its fragrance, I had no thought of turning back but rather approached to take it, if I dared to stretch my hand out to it. But sharp, stinging thistles kept me at a distance...'

problems. The dreamer walks beside a river and comes to the outside of this garden. It is enclosed by a square wall, on which are depicted hideous images representing various social vices. He gains admittance through a narrow gate, and finds himself in a paradise world peopled by courtly attributes. Later, the rose garden will be enclosed in a fortified castle, in order to protect the roses from being picked. The garden, spring and castle are, of course, characteristic *loci* of allegorical writing. But in GdL's text they are lacking in the spatial definition which would appear to be their primary function (*41*, pp.179-82). For example, the garden is glossed by C.S. Lewis as representing the world of the court, in which case the dreamer is inside the garden (*48*, p.119); but it is also possible to read the world of the garden as characterising the dreamer, in which case 'it' is (metaphorically) 'inside' him. By withholding the meaning of the dream, GdL leaves his major metaphors in suspension. The romance-like nature of his text allows them the possibility of not even being metaphors at all: on the literal level, they continue to constitute the landscape of quest.

The implications of many of these metaphors are criticised by the figure of Genius in JdM, who proposes a re-allegorisation of the garden to include meanings other than the simply erotic. But because Genius concentrates on the scene at the spring where the lover sees images reflected in the water, I shall defer discussion of this passage to Chapter 5, and consider here only how JdM responds to the central image of the rose. As I said above (p.16), he allows the dream an explicitly sexual conclusion. Venus casts her burning torch and the moment of consummation arrives at last. With a wink at others of 'love's pilgrims', the dreamer gets a serious attack of metaphor. He aims at an 'arrow slit' (presumably in Jalousie's castle) with his 'straight, strong pilgrim's staff' (21354 [21324]); he carries a 'pilgrim's bag' containing (incongruously) two 'hammers', more precious than musical instruments (21360 ff. [21330 ff.]). There follows a passage comparing the various kinds of 'ditch', 'path' or 'ford' (old, young, rich...) into which he has thrust his 'staff' (21397-21538 [21367-21508]). In an earlier passage the place of consummation had been compared with a sanctuary

containing a statue even more beautiful than Pygmalion's (20791-
20816 [20761-86]); and now the dreamer approaches it at last:

> De l'ymagete m'appressoi
> que du saintuaire pres soi;
> mout le baisai devotement,
> et por l'estuier sauvement
> veil mon bordon metre en l'archiere
> ou l'escharpe pendoit derriere.
> Bien le cuidai lancier de bout,
> mes il resort, et je rebout;
> mes riens ni vaut, ainçois recule,
> enrer [*read* entrer] n'i puet por chose nule
> car un palis dedens trovai
> que je bien sent, mes pas nel voi,
> dont l'archiere est dedens hordee
> des lors qu'el fu primes fondee.[*]
>
> (21601-14 [21571-84])

After a herculean struggle the obstacle is overcome, the dreamer
gets through the arrow slit and reaches... the rose bush. Seizing it by
the branches (or the flanks: there is a pun on OF *rains* 21705
[21675]) he goes for the bud:

> En la parfin, tant vous en di,
> un poi de grene y espandi,
> quant j'oi le bouton eslochié.
> Ce fu quant dedens l'oi tochié
> por les fueilletes reverchier,
> car je voloie tout cerchier
> jusques au fons du boutonet,

---

[*] 'I approached the statue which I knew to be close to the sanctuary. I
kissed it most piously and, in order to sheath my staff safely, I set about
inserting it into the arrow slit, with my bag hanging behind it. I meant to
thrust it in at once, but it comes back out, and I shove at it again; but it's no
good, it comes back out - nothing would make it go in, for I found a
palissade within, which I can clearly feel but not see, defending the arrow
slit from when it was first built.'

> si cum moi semble que bon est.
> Et fis lors si meller les grenes
> que se desmellassent a penes,
> si que tout le boutonnet tendre
> en fis eslargir et estendre.* (21719-30 [21689-700])

Clearly this passage is delighting in its own naughtiness. But it is also parodying GdL's rose metaphor in several ways. (1) Like thirteenth-century fabliaux-writers, JdM uses what has been termed 'obscene allegory' (*32*): a technique of writing which, although it pretends to use a euphemistic discourse about sex, is in fact more explicit and more 'improper' than literal or 'proper' language would have been (*17*, pp.85-90). The suggestion is that the mystery attaching to GdL's metaphor is mere mystification: the dreamer was really after sex, and produced sexual excitement through 'improper' naming of his lover's genital. (2) At the end of this hallucinatory metaphorical sequence – sacked castle, arrow slit, reliquary, statue – the return of the rose is like a return to the literal; and this draws attention to the tension between the metaphorical and the literal in GdL's poem. (3) The slippage from one metaphor to another that characterises this passage recalls the dreams and delusions conjured up by a lover's desire: erotic fantasy dictates perception, producing this burlesque mixture of the sensual and the religious.

All these three points have in common the doubt being cast over a 'higher' 'hidden' meaning. They suggest, on the contrary, that 'meaning' (such as it is) is limited by human sensual urges which, however, do nothing but delude us. To this extent, then, JdM's treatment of the 'allegorical' metaphor of GdL is ironic: rather than seeking *another* meaning beyond the text, he makes it difficult to see how we can attach any meaning to it with confidence.

---

* 'In the end, I tell you this much, I spilt a little of the seed into the bud, when I had shaken it. That was when I had felt it inside, turning back all the petals to search right to the bottom of it, as seems good. And then I caused the seeds to mingle, so that they could not be separated, so that I made the tender bud swell and expand.'

(iii) Personification

This third device of indirectness differs from the other two by its explicitness. The figures outside and within GdL's garden are all named after abstract qualities or defects, giving the text the air of pursuing a moral or psychological analysis. The range of characters is expanded by JdM to include some whose contribution is more explicitly political (Fausemblant) or philosophical (Nature, Genius). But both text and continuation seem possessed of an urge to inform, and this is illustrated by their choice of titles. GdL's prologue entitles it 'li *Romans de la Rose*, / ou l'art d'Amors est toute enclose' (37-38); JdM has Amor say it should be called 'le Miroër as amoreus, / tant i verront de bienz por eus' (10651-52 [10621-62]). (Both the terms 'art' and 'mirror' are frequently found in the titles of medieval didactic works.)

Personification allegory is both insistent and difficult for modern readers to come to terms with. To understand how it works, it is helpful to start with the character of Fausemblant. Hypocrisy incarnate, he is forever shifting ground; even his face, in a nightmarish descriptive detail, is 'white on the outside and black on the inside' (12013 [11983]) – less a face, indeed, than a mask. He loathes whatever is consistent:

> s'il sont tex genz cum il aperent,
> si net cum netement se perent,
> que lor dis s'acort a lor fais,
> n'est ce granz duelz et granz forfais?*
> (11931-34 [11901-04])

These words underline the 'proper' functioning of personification allegory: it should be perfectly consistent, so that a figure is the same inside and out, through and through. Thus GdL's figure of Biauté, who dances with Deduit, is beautiful in every respect; she

---

* '... if they are people such as they appear, as clean as they are cleanly groomed, their words attuned to their deeds, is that not a great shame and a great crime?'

has lovely qualities, a lovely face, lovely features and a lovely figure (990-1016). Richece, her neighbour in the dance, commands the respect of all (in OF *riche* means 'powerful' as well as 'wealthy'); she is envied and surrounded by flatterers; she wears elaborate clothes of imperial purple and drips with jewellery (1017-1108 [1017-1104]). The personification incarnates a general idea, and any particularity he or she may have should serve to illustrate that underlying 'form' or generality and make it visible.

     This device derives from religious writing seeking to explicate the moral and religious life (*39*, pp.118-30). It assumes a universality of experience. When, in a psychomachia, vices war with virtues, this is the moral experience of us all as we participate in Salvation History. In Poirion's phrase, 'l'allégorie fait déboucher la rhétorique sur la métaphysique' (*66*, p.11). Put crudely, the psychological model implied is that each human being resembles a bus with the same set of passengers all shouting directions to the driver. Some people go one way and others another, but as a result of interaction between the same impulses. In the dominant metaphor of such writing, each one of us is a battleground over which good and evil forces are at war.

     GdL's personifications are less philosophical than poetic. The generalities they embody constitute, collectively, the tradition of courtly poetry, in which this technique already had a century-long history, principally in the work of the troubadours (*40*, pp.122-169, *41*, pp.50-83). Thus when the dreamer enters the garden, he leaves behind him, depicted on its outer wall, a world represented as much socially as ethically: Haïne, Felonnie ('treachery'), Vilonnie ('uncourtliness'), Convoitise, Avarice, Envie, Viellece, Papelardie ('excessive, or hypocritical, piety') and Povreté. Indeed, as Kelly has pointed out, the descriptions of these statues reinforce each other: all the figures are ugly and harmful to nobility or *proece* (*45*, p.59). Conversely, the world the dreamer finds inside the garden, once he has been admitted by Oiseuse ('leisure'), is one of pleasured elegance: the figures in Deduit's dance are Leesce ('merriment'), Amor, Biauté, Richece, Verité, Largece, Franchise ('nobility of spirit'), Cortoisie, and Jonece. To redeploy the inherited vocabulary of the love lyric is to court irony: instead of representing metaphysical certainties, GdL's text is recycling a self-consciously poetic discourse whose relation to 'reality' in any sense is problematic.

Certainly the 'generalities' of the love lyric are much less general than those of religious discourse. *Fin'amor* is the province of a select élite, and it is the sense of initiation to such an élite that these opening scenes of the *Rose* convey. Indeed, the prologue to the poem has already implied that a unique history is here to be unfolded: the dreamer and the rose belong in a particular chapter of autobiography. This means that readers of GdL's personifications have constantly to ask themselves where, on the allegorical level, the figures are to be situated: do they characterise two individuals or do they construct a representative social environment? This question is most acute in the case of those who surround the rose. The complementary pair of Dangier ('rebuff') and Bel Acuel can easily be read as the hostility or receptivity of an individual love object to her lover, whilst Honte and Poor can be viewed as *her* fear and *her* sense of shame. On the other hand Jalousie and Malebouche seem rather to represent elements of the social scene that the lover has to contend with. The difficulty of 'placing' the figures means that the literal and allegorical levels of the romance cannot always be made to coincide (cf. *66*, pp.41 ff.).

The consistency which Fausemblant so dislikes can result, on the rhetorical level, in little more than amplified tautology; take the example of Biauté, who is ... beautiful. But GdL is too skilled a poet for this often to be the case. His technique of personification produces an elaboration of details that are not readily recuperated allegorically. This fictional excess is another instance of the non-coincidence of the literal and the allegorical. One of the most troubling figures in this respect is Oiseuse. There is a lengthy description of her physical beauty; she carries a mirror and her whole day's work consists in titivation (525-74 [523-72]). Does she thereby constitute a denunciation of Luxuria (lust, as one of the seven deadly sins) (*28*, p.75) or on the contrary, can she be identified with the love object (*49*, p.41)? Is her beauty meant to imply that leisure is a beautiful experience, or that leisured individuals can cultivate their beauty? Is there some connection between leisure and femininity? *Oiseuse* in OF can be either a feminine substantive, or an adjective in the feminine. Are women more leisurely than men, or does leisure in some way 'feminise', and is that a good thing or not?

Similar questions can be addressed to other figures. The participants in the dance are mostly paired in couples, and the major reason for this seems to be less to stress the interrelation between pairs of ideas (if Deduit and Leesce make sense together, 'pleasure' and 'merriment' going hand in hand, what of Richece and Verité?) than to suggest by fictional example that the garden is a place of courtship and love. This pairing raises the issue of gender. GdL's figures usually have the gender of the abstract noun they personify; yet when scenes of courtship are evoked, (grammatical) gender becomes overlaid with ideas of (bodily) sex. (This is an implication which JdM will seize on; see below, p.30.) Furthermore, since most abstract nouns are feminine in OF, GdL's garden contains more women than men. The profusion of beautiful women that present themselves to the dreamer's gaze thus anticipates, again in exemplary form, the possibility of choosing one rose from among many. And to provide partners for these women, GdL introduces 'real' men: Largece has as companion a knight of Arthur's lineage (1176-77 [1174-75]), Franchise a son of the lord of Windsor (1224-28 [1222-26]). Such 'people' are out of place in this garden of personifications, and again, call interpretation into question.

GdL himself admits the shortcomings of his chosen mode as the 'plot' of the 'romance' advances. The stationary figures on the wall can easily achieve consistency since they are not called upon to act. The dance which Deduit leads is a kind of *tableau mouvant*, as though the wall outside the garden were matched by a moving one within it; again, the figures are not tempted out of conformity with their 'natures'. But when the dreamer starts to court the rose, the personifications have to react. Sometimes the literal and the figurative plots work well in harness, as in the account of the construction of Jalousie's castle (3802ff. [3784ff.]). Anxious to keep the influential Luxure and Licherie away from the roses (3601-07 [3583-89]), she imprisons Bel Acuel in a fortress the four corner towers of which are guarded by Dangier, Honte, Poor and Malebouche. The repression of female receptivity by social and moral control, so as to avoid sexual contamination, is here graphically portrayed. At other times, however, the literal and figurative plots strain against each other, as when the figures around the rose have to enact the play of receptivity and rebuff. Bel Acuel and Dangier have to alternate; but each also has to prepare for the arrival of the other by 'changing' character. Thus Bel Acuel becomes 'dangerous', for which he is reproached by Venus (3442ff. [3424ff.]), whilst Dangier becomes welcoming and is reproved by Honte:

> Il n'afiert pas a vostre non
> que vos faciés se dangier non.
> Se Bel Acuel est frans et dous,
> et vous soiés fel et estous,
> et plains de rampone et d'outrage.* (3695-99 [3677-81])

Thus although GdL's *Rose* draws on a didactic tradition of explicit allegory, his personifications – like his metaphor of the rose – are ambiguously strung between the figurative and the literal. The resulting text is teasing, intangible, and altogether charming.

Whereas GdL's main technique of personification is description, JdM uses speech. His continuation consists largely of harangues by his six major characters, of whom Raison, Ami and la Vielle were briefly introduced by GdL, and who are now joined by Fausemblant, Nature and Genius. In GdL's *Rose*, as we saw, the personifications equivocate between representing the world of a social élite, and a chapter of individual autobiography. JdM inflates the field of the allegory to the cosmic, and so blows this courtly framework apart. Ami and la Vielle explicate male and female amorous experience; Raison, Nature, and Genius are, compared

---

* 'It isn't appropriate to your name that you should be other than rebuffing. Bel Acuel's role is to be open and welcoming, and you should be violent and bold, full of insults and outrage.'

with the dreamer at least, giants of intellect who survey a vast range of human possibilities. Insect-like, the dreamer continues to concentrate his puny strength on the pursuit of one single object – the rose – but in so doing he becomes a kind of serio-comic exemplar of human inadequacy. The idea that the personifications could be in some sense 'inside' him is much harder to sustain than in GdL's *Rose*; their relationship to him is not always clear, but the model which is most widely applicable is that of teachers to (unwilling) pupil.

For reasons such as this, Lewis dismissed JdM as an inept allegorist (*48*, pp.137 ff.). I would contend, however, that JdM saw in GdL's use of personification a kind of literary brinkmanship: how far can the device be pushed before it collapses back into the literal? Such risk-taking is altogether to his taste; he plays the same game, but more audaciously. Let me illustrate this by looking again at Fausemblant. This epitome of unreliability serves as a warning to all readers of all texts, but especially to those of the *Rose*. His message, 'trust me, nothing is as it seems', is clearest at the end of his speech, when he volunteers his services to Amor:

> 'Mes a vous n'ose je mentir;
> mes se je peüsse sentir
> que vous ne la perceüssiés,
> la mençonge ou poing eüssiés;
> certainnement je vous boulasse,
> ja por pechié ne le lessasse;
> si vous porré je bien faillir,
> se vous m'en deviés mal baillir.'
> Li diex sorrist de la merveille,
> chascuns s'en rist et s'en merveille,
> et dient 'Ci a biau sergent
> ou bien se doivent fier gent!'[*]   (11969-80 [11939-50])

---

[*] ' "But I dare not lie to you; though if I were able to feel that you would not perceive it you would get a fistful of lies; and I would certainly trick you, undeterred by thoughts of sin; and I could certainly betray you if you were to do me harm." The god [Amor] smiled at the marvel, and everyone

Amor then asks if Fausemblant will keep his word, and he promises:

> 'Oïl, je vous jur et fiance,
> n'onc n'orent sergent plus leal
> vostre peres ne vostre eal.'
> 'Comment? c'est contre ta nature.'
> 'Metés vous en aventure,
> car se pleges en requerriés,
> ja plus a seür n'en seriés.'* (11986-92 [11956-62])

The self-consciousness of this allegory surpasses that of GdL, presenting us with the conundrum of the hypocrite who unmasks himself, and so solicits belief, and yet remains a hypocrite, and so places himself beyond it. This double move is reiterated throughout JdM's text which both constantly solicits its readers' complicity and yet also undermines itself. In Fausemblant, in other words, the two issues addressed by this chapter, allegory and irony, converge.

Fausemblant's favourite pose is that of a mendicant friar. He is accompanied by a sinister woman figure called Contrainte Abstinence. (Her name apparently means that she is not truly chaste, but either withholds from sexual activity because she has to, or else gives a false appearance of doing so.) They help the dreamer by gaining entry to Jalousie's castle and persuading Malebouche to repent of having slandered him. When the penitent kneels down they strangle him and cut out his tongue; henceforth his section of the fortifications is unguarded. This grisly scene is an accomplished piece of allegorical writing, indicating that the most effective way to combat jealousy is to silence slander by means of hypocrisy (Fausemblant) and sexual deceit (Contrainte Abstinence). But there are other games being played out here too. The text of

---

laughs and is astonished, saying, "Here's a fine henchman and thoroughly trustworthy!"'

* '"Yes, I swear and pledge that your father and grandfather never had so loyal a servant." "How so? It's contrary to your nature." "Take your chance, for if you were to ask for pledges, that wouldn't make you any more secure."'

Fausemblant's sermon is the truism that 'one should keep a watch
on one's tongue'; failure to do so on Malebouche's part means that
he literally loses his. The truism is borrowed from the long
discourse of Raison (cf. 12179-86 [12149-56] and 7037 [7007]), and
its appearance in Fausemblant's mouth undermines Raison's
authority, just as his citing the dreamer's behaviour as evidence of
his innocent intent towards the rose reminds us that this behaviour
was based on Ami's advice (cf. 12277-12326 [12247-96] and 7308-
50 [7278-320]). Fausemblant's false-seeming thereby draws the
previous speakers into its web.

     He is also important as a satirical figure, attacking the
mendicant orders and contemporary problems at the University of
Paris. In this respect, he has to be read literally as well as
allegorically. Indeed, JdM encourages confusion between his
personifications and 'people'. I said above (p.26) that he inherits
from GdL a certain interplay between sex and gender. This is used
for comic effect with both Raison and Nature. Raison, trying to
dissuade the dreamer from the service of Amor, proposes that he
should love her instead; this philosophic prospect is, however,
immediately burlesqued by her identification with the 'typical'
woman who cannot bear to be scorned. Her 'fille sui Dieu le sovrain
pere' (5816 [5786]) gives way to 'trop sont dolentes et confuses /
puceles qui sont refusees' (5834-35 [5804-05]). Similarly Nature is
confused for a time with a garrulous and untrustworthy woman; in
Genius's eyes she passes from being 'du monde roïne, / cui toute
rienz mondaine encline' (16295-96 [16265-66]) to being included
in a denunciation of all women as being stupid and unstable:
'decevable et nices, / et de flechissable nature' (16342-43 [16312-
13]). (This confusion of Nature with a 'mere' woman is also found
in JdM's sources, Alan of Lille's *Plaint of Nature*, 8, pp.108-09;
and cf. 77, pp.281-82.)

     Genius's 'consolation' of Nature is ironic, both in that it is
hardly comforting to be subjected to a misogynist tirade, and that he
himself concedes its irrelevance, concluding:

          Si n'ai je pas por vous ce dit,
          car vous avés, sans contredit,

touz jors esté loialz et ferme.
L'escriture neïs afferme
tant vous en donne Diex san fin,
que vous estes [sages] san fin.* (16701-06 [16671-76])

Genius, then, has not said quite what he meant to say; he has been
rambling. This he has in common with JdM's other personifications, who constantly stray from the point. Raison is the first,
and in some ways most worrying, example of this.

Indeed, Raison is the first real test of the reader's patience.
I admit to finding her boring. She herself recognises the danger of
being longwinded (6184-89 [6154-59], 6738-40 [6708-10]); the
dreamer is exhausted by her tirade (7225 [7195]). Her message is
simple: give up Amor, to serve whom is folly, and adopt a more
rational approach to life. However, she harps so on the 'follies' to be
shunned as to give them far more prominence than what she in fact
recommends (*64*, pp.8-9). This is not just a matter of defining
things by their opposites, despite the dreamer's suggestion that
understanding operates through contraries: 'les unes sont des autres
gloses, / et qui l'une en veut defenir, / de l'autre li doit sovenir
(21574-76 [21544-46]: 'opposites gloss each other, to define one
you must recall the other'). Instead, Raison's discourse is constantly
being deflected sideways in such a way as to undermine, rather than
reinforce, her position. Thus for example she starts by
recommending *bon' amor;* but when the dreamer objects that such
ideal love is unrealistic, she recommends a diluted form of it in
which you do as you would be done by; then she undermines the
likelihood even of that by detailing social institutions whose purpose
it is to remedy the *lack* of such friendship; and from there she goes
on to illustrate how justice is corrupt... The more she argues, the
further she is carried away from her original point. This slippage in
Raison's speech exaggerates a tendency already present in GdL's
Raison, who finds herself giving a disquisition on *folie* (2998 ff.

---

* 'But I didn't say this on your account for you have assuredly always been
loyal and steadfast. Scripture goes so far as to affirm that God has given
you such subtle understanding that you are infinitely wise.'

[2982 ff.]). One can analyse a similar drift in the other figures; Ami, for instance, seems to be less of a true friend than the man who remained loyal to the dreamer in his destitution (cf. *77*, pp.280-81). Thus, though we might expect JdM's cosmic figures to be more 'metaphysical' than GdL's courtly fictions, they tend, like Fausemblant, to look rather hollow, more like ironic masks than real faces.

It should be clear that although this is the end of the chapter it is by no means the end of the subject. The provocation to interpret, and its frustration, are the condition of reading the *Romance of the Rose*. This chapter has tried to indicate some of the ways in which these contradictory impulses operate in the text, not to resolve or reconcile them. This will be immediately evident when we consider the use of first-person perspective in the next chapter.

3. Voice and Writing

So far I have referred to the protagonist of the *Rose* as 'the dreamer'. The purpose of this chapter is to describe more fully the poem's use of a first-person voice, and its implications.

First-person interventiôn is rare in medieval romances, apart from a few where the narrator interpolates fragments of his own courtship into the predominantly third-person narrative of his hero (*Li Biaus Desconneüs, Partonopeu de Blois, Joufroi de Poitiers*). Thus, although immeasurably longer than typical examples of either, the *Rose* must be compared with the two major first-person genres of thirteenth-century France: the lyric and the *dit*. Lyric poems on the theme of love, sung by a performer who enacts the first-person character of author and lover, had been composed in Northern France since about the 1160s and were a well-established and prestigious genre at the time GdL was writing. The *dit*, in comparison, is composed to be narrated or read; its tone is often satirical or burlesque; its emergence is a thirteenth-century phenomenon, a major author in the genre being JdM's contemporary Rutebeuf (died c. 1285).

In recent years, the *dit* has been the object of two important studies. Michel Zink concentrates on the difference between the first-person subject of a *dit* and that of the courtly lyric (*80*, pp.47-79). The lyric focuses attention on what is typical, or abstract and ideal, in the love experience; it may hint at autobiographical incident, but only to illustrate the relation of the lover to the exemplary. The *dit*, by contrast, takes up this potential for anecdotal autobiography and makes it its principal subject matter. (By 'autobiography' I mean 'telling a life from a first-person perspective'; I don't mean to imply that it need be truthful.) The *je* of the *dit* is theatrical, often comic; it has been the butt of insult or humiliation; it belongs in particular historical circumstances. This means that it discourages identification with it by the audience, who are more likely to laugh at it than to feel with it. The *je* of the *dit* is thereby contrasted with that of the lyric, which invites audience complicity. Jacqueline Cerquiglini, in the second of these two studies, defines the *dit* as above all 'une méta-écriture' (*22*, p.155), or an instance of writing about writing, because despite its concessions to narrative it more closely resembles a compilation: it is a 'montage', a splicing together of different kinds of discourse. Although the *dit* retains a trace of the oral (its name designates it as a 'telling'), this montage effect implies acknowledgement of written models such as the compendium or manual. Thus whereas Zink sees the first-person teller of the *dit* as a kind of stand-up comic, Cerquiglini sees him as a professional writer. 'Le *je* qui apparaît dans le *dit* n'est pas le *je* indifférencié, universel de la lyrique courtoise. [...] Il fait référence à un type social' (*22*, p.164): the type, precisely, of a compiler or composer of manuals, that is to say, a clerk. (On the clerk as a scholar or intellectual, rather than as someone who embraces the religious life, see *53*, p.264.)

To anyone familiar with the *Rose*, it will already be obvious how suggestive these characterisations are for comparing GdL's text, whose debt to the lyric tradition has been widely noted, with that of JdM, so much more a clerkly compiler and cultivator of 'low' comedy. As I examine their work in this light, however, I shall argue (as in the last chapter) that JdM is receptive to elements in GdL's text, and elaborates upon them. He does not crudely stick a *dit* on to a lyric any more than he could be said suddenly to switch from allegory to irony. His text, insofar as it is a *dit*, can of course accommodate lyricism as one discourse among others in the compilation. Keeping the lyric and the *dit* in mind as reference points, I shall discuss the use of the first person in the *Rose* under three headings: autobiography, subjectivity, and the role of writing.

(i) Autobiography

Autobiography typically involves at least two meanings of the first person: 'I' (here and now) recount the actions and reactions of 'I' (in the past). This is exactly how GdL's *Rose* begins. Commenting ('now') on the truthfulness of dreams, he recounts one from his own past:

> Ou vintieme an de mon aage
> ou point qu'Amors prent le paage
> des jones gens, couichez estoie
> une nuit, si cum je souloie;
> et me dormoie mout forment;
> lor vi un songe en mon dorment...* (21-26)

We return to 'now' as he states his intention of composing an 'art of Love' in honour of 'her who is worthy of being called rose' (34-44), before reverting to the past:

> Avis m'estoit qu'il estoit maiz,
> il a ja bien cinq ans ou maiz;
> en may estions, si songoie
> ou temps amorous plain de joie...** (45-48)

He goes on to recount what he saw in the dream, thereby introducing a dream 'I'. The first person, from now on, has three distinct referents: GdL as author and admirer of a rose-like dedicatee; the same person, five years previously; and the fantasy-self within the dream. (This analysis follows, with slight modification, that of Vitz, *76*, pp.49-54.)

As Vitz observes, such distinctions make it possible for the autobiographical text to play off different perspectives against each other, but GdL does not pursue this option. On the contrary, his text tends to blur the distinctions and affirm, instead, the narrator's solidarity with his former self and his fantasy self. For example, in the passages just quoted, the season of May and its connection with love serve to conflate rather than distinguish the various 'selves'. Now, when love takes its toll, he dreams of five years ago when it

---

* 'In the twentieth year of my life, when Love takes its toll of the young, I was lying down one night, as usual; I was fast asleep, and then, in my sleep, I saw a dream...'

** 'It seemed to me that it was May, five years ago or more; we were in May, and I was dreaming in the joyful, amorous season...'

was May in his dream, the time for love (45, 48), and perhaps May as he dreamt (47); or else he remembers now, when love takes its toll, a dream he had five years ago when it was May (46-47) and he dreamt of May, the time for love. (On the confusing chronology of this prologue, see *80*, p.128.) Rather than exploring the potential for multiple perspectives of autobiography, his romance thus presents a unified 'character' of narrator, dreamer and lover, which resembles the composite author-lover-singer of a lyric poem (cf. *41*, pp.138-145).

As the fiction progresses, we become less conscious of any narrating voice external to the dream, and concentrate increasingly on the fantasy self – the 'I' *within* the dream. This dream self is the closest of the three to the timeless, emotion-torn voice of the lyric poet. A careful reading of the whole of GdL's *Rose* alongside poems by the early troubadours persuades Leslie Topsfield that 'the process of falling in love and of submission to Love in the *Rose* is [...] expressed in terms which a thirteenth-century audience would immediately associate with the courtly love lyric and the situation in which the troubadour or trouvère pleads for mercy with his lady' (*73*, p.45). When GdL's text breaks off, it is in a love lament which is almost indistinguishable, apart from its form, from a courtly love song. Here are its last lines, in which the first-person voice apostrophises the imprisoned and absent Bel Acuel:

> Par un poi que je ne fons d'ire
> quant il me membre de la perte
> qui est si grant et si aperte.
> Si en ai duel et desconfort,
> qui me donroit, ce croi, la mort.
> Las! j'en doi bien avoir poor
> quant je sé que losengeor
> et traïtour et envious
> sont de moi nuire curious...

Jamés n'iert riens qui m'en confort
se je pers vostre bien voillance,
car je n'ai mes aillors fiance.*
(4038-46, 4056-58 [4010-18, 4026-28])

This poet-lover, on the verge of death from sorrow, hounded by slanderers and appealing to the goodwill of his lady as his only resource, recalls singers from the heyday of lyric composition, such as Bernart de Ventadorn and Gace Brulé.

We saw in the last chápter how GdL's use of allegory confuses the boundary between the 'self' and 'society'. In the lyric, likewise, the individual and the social are not clearly distinguished, because the lover-protagonist of a lyric poses as an exemplary figure whose words resume the beliefs of the sympathetic audience. Here is an illustration of this from a song by the thirteenth-century trouvère Adam de la Halle:

On demande mout souvent k'est Amors,
dont mains hons est dou respondre abaubis,
mais ki a droit sent les douces dolors
par soi meïsme en puet estre garnis –
u pas n'aime, ce m'est vis;
et, s'il aime, s'est la vie
en celui mal emploïe
ki vit en si fole error,
car il dist k'il a seignor
et si ne le connoist mie.**   (6, XIII, 1-10)

---

* 'When I recall this loss, so great and so evident, I almost melt with distress. And I feel grief and sorrow which I believe might kill me. Alas, I am right to fear, when I know that tale-bearers, traitors and envious men are intent on injuring me... I shall never be consoled if I lose your good will, for there is no one else to whom I commit my trust.'

** 'People often ask what love is, which makes many at a loss how to reply, but whoever properly feels its sweet pains can provide the answer from his own experience, or else, it seems to me, he is not in love; and if he does love, then he is wasting his time to be living in such foolish confusion as to say that he has a lord [i.e. Love], but does not know at all who he is.'

Adam puts those who ask him about the nature of love in the wrong, for one of two reasons: either they are not in love (and so, by implication, their question is irrelevant) or else they are, in which case it is inconceivable they should be ignorant of that which dominates their lives. The lyric singer speaks to other lovers, and on their behalf, telling them what they already know. In a similar way, the 'I' of GdL's *Rose* is both an individual lover, and a representative of all courtly lovers (cf. *76*, p.59). The dream 'I' abandons himself to love in what sounds like a declaration of individual passion; for example:

> Vous poés ce que vous vodrois
> fere de moi, pendre ou tuer;
> bien sai que je ne puis muer,
> car ma vie est en vostre main.
> Ne puis vivre jusqu'a demain,
> se n'est par vostre volenté.
> J'atens par vous avoir santé,
> car ja par autre ne l'avré.*   (1904-11 [1902-9])

But this effusion prompts, on Amors' part, the longest speech of GdL's text (2023-764 [2021-748]) in which the commandments of love for *all* lovers are set forth, the typical sufferings of lovesickness detailed, and their three universal palliatives – Dous Penser, Dous Parler, and Dous Regart – prescribed. The two themes, announced in the prologue, of individual courtship and 'Art' of love, are here emphatically combined.

This exemplary character of the lover means that whether the autobiographical experiences he speaks of actually took place is less important than their desirability for those who share his views. In both lyric and *Rose* as GdL conceived it, such exemplariness is class-specific: only the 'courtly' individual can find his autobiography, whether actual, potential, or fantasised, reflected in that of the *Rose* protagonist. As was pointed out in the last chapter (pp.24-

---

* 'You can do what you choose with me, hang me or strike me down, I cannot alter, for my life is in your hand. I cannot live until tomorrow unless by your will. I look to you for health, for no one else will give it to me.'

25), the personifications in the first part of the *Rose* present social as much as ethical values. Poverty and rusticity are on the wall outside; the figures within are described in such a way as to imply that social status confers beauty and desirability, and vice versa. GdL's text thereby echoes the programmatic opposition of *vilain* and *courtois* in the courtly lyric. The garden of love, guarded by Oiseuse and presided over by Deduit, is reserved for those whose conspicuous consumption of time denies them any occupation other than joining the dance of pleasure.

GdL, then, presents us with a first-person lover-narrator modelled on the autobiographical stance of the medieval love lyric. How does JdM respond to the first-person figure created by his predecessor?

His most flamboyant gesture is to undo the solidarity of the first-person. Amor wants to help the dreamer, and starts by regretting that Gallus, Catullus and Ovid, masters on the subject of love, are no longer available to offer advice:

> Mes chascuns d'euz gist mors porris.
> Ves ci Guillaume de Lorris
> cui Jalousie, sa contraire,
> fait tant d'angoisse et de mal traire
> qu'il est en peril de morir
> se ne pensons du secorir.* (10525-29 [10495-10500])

This naming of Guillaume de Lorris provides the only identification which we have of the poet of the first part of the *Rose*, and as the subsequent development of Amor's speech shows, it is no accident that he is named in the company of poets who are *mors porris*. Reviewing his efforts on the dreamer's behalf, Amor recalls that Guillaume too has served him:

> si a commencié ce romans
> ou seront mis touz mes commans

---

* 'But they all lie dead and rotten. Here is Guillaume de Lorris, whom Jalousie, his opponent, subjects to so much anguish and suffering that he's in danger of death unless we take steps to help him.'

> et jusques la le finera
> ou il a Bel Acuel dira...
> 'Jamés n'iert riens qui me confort
> se je pers vostre bien voillance,
> car je n'ai mes aillors fiance.'*
>   (10549-52, 10558-60 [10519-22, 10528-30])

Lines 10555-60 [10525-30] are an exact quotation of 4053-58 [4023-28], the last lines attributed (on the strength of this passage) to GdL. According to Amor they are yet to be written (see the future tenses in the opening lines of the quotation above); and after writing them, Guillaume will die. The autobiographical fiction which subtends the first part of the *Rose* is being dismantled here. The dreamer and fantasy-lover are being split apart from the author, whose activity is jocularly assigned to the future by Amor, although it is obvious to the reader that it has already taken place! Amor goes on to introduce a new author-figure, Jean, who will be born at Meun-sur-Loire, and will be a great devotee of love:

> Cis avra le romans si chier,
> qu'il le vodra tout parfenir...
> ans trespassés plus de quarente,
> et dira por la mescheance,
> por poor de desesperance
> qu'il ait de Bel Acuel perdue
> la bien veillance avant eüe:
> 'Et si l'ai je perdue, espoir,
> a poi que ne me desespoir',
> et toutes les autres paroles
> qu'eles que soient, sages ou foles,
> jusqu'a tant qu'il avra coillie
> sus la branche vert et foillie
> la tres bele rose vermeille

---

* '... and he has begun this romance where all my commands will be set down, and he will finish up to the point where he says to Bel Acuel, [...] "I shall never be consoled if I lose your good will, for there is no one else to whom I commit my trust."'

> et qu'il soit jors et qu'il s'esveille.*
> (10584-5, 10590-10602 [10554-55, 10560-72])

Lines 10595-96 are a repetition of 4059-60 [4029-30], the opening lines (on this authority) of Jean's continuation, whilst the very last lines of the quotation approximate to its closing lines of the whole romance. Just as Amor's speech at the centre of what we have of GdL's text crystallises the meaning of the first part of the romance, so his speech at the centre of the continued one embraces the whole of the continued work. (The idea that the midpoint of a medieval work is especially significant, and in some way focuses its meaning, has been defended with reference to a variety of texts; the relevance of the midpoint to the *Rose* was first sugested by Uitti, *75*, pp.112-14, and is explored in more detail by Sylvia Huot, *37*, pp.72, 90-94.) But whereas Amor in GdL shows the autobiographical self to be typical, an aristocratic Everyman, in JdM his central speech sabotages the whole autobiographical framework by blowing narrator, dreamer and dream-self wide apart. The fiction of the dream is undermined as well, since a character in a dream tells the dreamer of that dream that he will be superseded by another; and tells him so in terms which make it clear that he already has been! The dream has been highjacked by another dreamer; and the text has been highjacked by a different author. To round off the joke, Amor prays to the goddess of childbirth to assure Jean's safe delivery into this world! It becomes impossible to believe in the text as an autobiography, even a fictional one.

The rubricators of some *Rose* MSS distinguish by marginal rubrics *L'Auctor* from *L'Amant*, and in some cases identify the first instances of this split in GdL (*37*, pp.91-95). But the gap between 'narrator' and 'lover' is far wider in JdM than it was in GdL. In his

---

* 'He will like the romance so much that he will set about finishing it to the end, [...] more than forty years later. And he will say, at the misfortune, for fear of despairing at having lost the favour of Bel Acuel which was previously his, "And if I have maybe lost it, I am almost driven to despair". And then [he will say] all the other things, wise or foolish, until the time he picks from the green and leafy branch the beautiful scarlet rose, and day comes, and he awakes.'

text, furthermore, both change character radically. The lover ceases
to be a noble, courtly youth and becomes instead a dissembling
sensualist. I have already quoted (p.20) the passage where he boasts
of his achievements with his 'pilgrim's staff'. But the rot had set in
well before this; even before this scene with Amor we recognise that
the lover is no longer the man we thought he was. Primed by the
cynical advice on seduction given him by Ami, he tries to bring
down Jalousie's castle by going down the path of Trop Doner, but
he is prevented from entering it by Richece, on the grounds that he's
too poor. In other words, the lover has tried to buy his way to
success, and only fails because he lacks the means. Disconsolate, he
resolves on deceit as the only means open to him (10303-06 [10273-
76]). Amor extracts from him the assurance that he is still
committed to winning the rose, despite his long conversation with
Raison, and he replies:

> Or vuel, sanz plus Raison ensivre,
> en vostre loi morir et vivre.
> [...]
> Atropos morir ne me doigne
> fors en fesant vostre besoigne,
> ainçois me prengne dedens l'euvre
> dont Venus plus volentiers euvre.*
>   (10367-68, 10370-74 [10337-38, 10340-44])

Such a wish betrays a departure from the innocent idealism of the
lover in GdL. In JdM the lover also stops occupying the central
ground in the narrative. Subjected as he is to lengthy tirades on this
and that, he – as a specimen of desiring humanity – becomes more
the comic butt, and the matter under discussion, of the
personifications, whose debate is carried on over his head. For
instance, he seems quite incapable of taking in much of Raison's
speech, responding only to what he sees as her use of a rude word

---

* 'Now I intend, following Raison no longer, to live and die in your law.
May Atropos [one of the Fates, responsible for determining when one dies]
not give me death except while I am executing your task; let him take me in
the work at which Venus is most pleased to occupy herself.'

(6901-42 [6871-912]). This serio-comic figure has more in common
with the protagonist of the *dit* as described by Zink: no longer
'noble', he combines stupidity with sensuality, and is unlikely to
command the admiring identification of an audience.

The figure of the narrator, however, moves in a different
direction, and one which corresponds with Cerquiligni's account of
the first person in the *dit* as clerk-compiler. Again, this is not
entirely an innovation on JdM's part since the narrator in GdL is
evidently familiar with poetry in the style of Ovid, and opens his
text with a conventional, learned romance prologue; he, however,
wears his learning lightly, whereas JdM is forever quoting and
naming learned sources (see below). This constant clerical self-
advertisement seems to win the approval of Nature, who explicitly
defends the superiority of the scholar's character over that of the
aristocrat:

> Si ront clerc plus grant avantage
> d'estre cortois, gentis et sage,
> (et la raison vous en liroi)
> que n'ont li prince ne li roy
> qui ne sevent de lettreüre:
> car li clers voit en l'escriture...
> touz maus don l'en se doit retraire
> et touz les bienz que l'en doit faire.*
>   (18635-40, 18643-44 [18605-10, 18613-14])

The only worthwhile qualities, she continues, are those which
inhere in the individual: a lack of moral distinction is worse in those
with inherited rank than in those of low birth, since we admire
people more for their own achievements than for advantages derived
from family background (cf. *53*, pp.270-81, 350-55). Nature is
implicitly criticising GdL's protagonist, who is apparently born to a
life of idleness, which he complacently equates with worth

---

* 'And furthermore learned men have a better chance of being courtly,
noble and wise than do kings or princes have who cannot read, and I'll tell
you why: for the learned man sees in books [...] all the ills one should shun,
all the good things one should do.'

('courtliness'). Immediately before this, Nature has compared kings
with paintings: both, she says, look better from a distance (18570-78
[18540-48]). This recalls the opening of GdL's text, where the
narrator studies the images on the wall, and reads their
accompanying labels. Perhaps Nature is implying that the aspiring
courtier reads less well than the clerk, and that the images of
uncourtliness on the wall, like those of royalty, exercise a certain
trompe-l'œil.

(ii) Subjectivity

Autobiography involves first-person narration of aspects of a 'life',
and we have seen that the unified experience of the aristocratic
teller of GdL's *Rose* breaks down in JdM's continuation, where
there is a comic disjunction between a foolish and sensual lover and
a learned narrator. The term 'subjectivity' is used in critical writing
to detach the first-person position from such autobiographical
appendages as social rank, which situates the subject as a *person*, in
order to examine, instead, the position of the first person in
language, or in a particular discourse, and the perspective which it
offers.

In the lyric, the first-person subject is positioned within a
traditional discourse, or register of language. If a poet does not use
this register, his compositions will not be recognisable as lyric; he is
subject to these conventions, which pre-exist him. By using
personification allegory. GdL emphasises this aspect of lyric
subjectivity. The first person remains nameless but moves among
animated names which incarnate the vocabulary of lyric discourse
and which, through their interactions with the subject, help to locate
him (*41*, pp.171-72, 179-83). The very generality of lyric discourse
means that the subject is to a great extent defined by participation in
the social rituals of 'courtliness'. Lyric language, as we have seen,
fosters community, not individualism. As a result, the position of
the individual in language is never clearcut. Social discourse
determines our subjectivity, but in so doing deprives us of any sense
of being uniquely ourselves.

What principally serves to focus the subject in GdL's poem is desire for the object: the rose. Like the subject, the object is unnamed. But whereas the subject interacts with language, as represented by the various personifications, the rose is an object, it belongs in the domain of nature (see 2913-14 [2897-98]) and remains, with that disconcerting literalism discussed in the last chapter, a flower. The subject wants to pick this flower. By representing the object of his desire in this way, he outdoes the traditional lyric in which the beloved, a lady, is presented as being at least potentially a subject: she may decide to reward or penalise; she may speak to the lover, or at least look at him. In the *Rose*, the personifications which occupy the rose garden seem to relate only to the subjectivity of the lover, or to some nameless force of social control of which the rose, as mere object, is oblivious. Thus Dangier and Bel Acuel are responses to the lover's desire, Poor and Honte are containing pressures. The rose has no voice and no subject position in any discourse. The lover as subject may be frustrated, unhappy and lamenting, but at least he is not competing for the first-person position. He's guaranteed a certain success, even if he fails in his quest for the rose: he commands the text.

This security is underwritten by the way gender is organised in this part of the *Rose*. Subjectivity, GdL's poem suggests, is a masculine prerogative; or, more properly, a male one, since the lover's desire is reinforced by parallels with other *men*: with Narcissus, who loved and died at the Fontainne d'Amor where the dreamer first sees the rose; and with Ami, the friend who counsels him. Two forces compete unequally for the allegiance of this masculine world, Amor and Raison. Although Raison loses, she at least shows that men have minds; the rose does not. And Amor, who makes by far the longest speech in GdL, is an articulate ideologue. Feminine desire is scarcely contemplated in this text. It is evoked briefly in the figure of Echo (who is censured for causing Narcissus's downfall) and identified, briefly again, with Venus, whose flaming torch has aroused many women (3424-26 [3406-08]). But Venus is an altogether marginal figure in comparison with Amor, and her single attribute, her torch, places her in a domain of elemental forces, outside (or beneath) language.

Denying the beloved subjectivity is, however, something of an impediment to courtship. It is not surprising, then, that GdL's *Rose* ends by resorting to the same solution as the lyric: that of masculinising the beloved. In lyric poetry, the lady is endowed with the social powers of lordship (bestowing fiefs, adjudicating in courts of law, waging war) which, in historical reality, were the prerogatives of men. In the *Rose*, the love object is gradually identified with, and thus displaced by, one principal personification, Bel Acuel. Like the lover, Bel Acuel is a young man, and yet to him the lover addresses what we have seen to be 'love poetry' (see above, pp.36-37). The rose can become a subject only if it is replaced by a masculine entity, created in the image of the lover, a projection of his desire, and a response to it. By increasingly directing courtship towards Bel Acuel, GdL's text shows the extent to which 'courtly love' is powered by homosocial desire, that is, desire by men for the values (such as status) they find only in other men.

JdM's text presents a complex response to the problems of subjectivity and gender raised by GdL. We saw in the previous chapter that in the dénouement he allows sexual imagery to run riot. The object of desire is in a constant state of flux, as the burlesque lover seems to keep forgetting whether he is storming a castle, sticking his 'staff' into a 'ditch', worshipping at a shrine – or picking a rose. A more radical change in the nature of the love object takes place in the story of Pygmalion's figurine. Pygmalion has made an extraordinarily beautiful statue (it is compared with the 'figure' in the 'sanctuary' where the 'pilgrim' wants to 'worship') and then fallen in love with it. There is an exuberantly comic description of his attempts to woo this unresponsive object of his own making. All the resources of art are called into play: music, poetry, dancing, dress-making... In the end, Venus takes pity on Pygmalion and gives the statue life. The object becomes a person, and, shortly afterwards, a mother!

This scene offers a commentary on 'courtly' behaviour which is both burlesque and shrewd. Like Pygmalion, GdL's lover is infatuated with a literal object, and woos it with the lyricist's 'art'.

The last thing he wants is to see the rose transformed into a person: he is much happier waiting to pick it and, while he waits, talking with Bel Acuel. His fictions of courtship, like Pygmalion's frenzy, are completely unproductive. It is not masculine art but the power of Venus, that is, of feminine desire, which can achieve consummation. The power of Venus, severely constrained in GdL's fiction, becomes in JdM a redoutable force. The Pygmalion story has been interpreted in various ways (see notably *26*, pp.106-07, 110-11; *37*, pp.97-99; *65*, p.159), but amongst other things, I think it derides the inadequacy of masculine art, and masculine fantasy, when they join forces to confine women in the role of object. The Vielle's long speech to Bel Acuel about women's sexual experience has, indeed, already dispelled the easy assumption that women are *not* knowing and desiring subjects. It is only Venus's intervention which brings about the collapse of Jalousie's castle. The riot of metaphor in the last pages of JdM is the last folly on the lover's part, and shows him still comically resolved on treating women as objects, regardless of the teachings of the text in which he figures.

JdM, then, can be seen as criticising, and burlesquing, courtly discourse that objectifies women and promotes the desiring male subject to a position of privilege. Instead, he opens up a wide range of different subject positions. The division introduced between 'narrator' and 'lover', discussed above, is one source of this diversity. Another is the proliferation of speakers, which contributes yet further perspectives from which an 'I' is heard. This polyphonic character of JdM's *Rose* is one of the principal sources of irony within it: it is hard for the reader to know if any of these conflicting voices possesses the authority to be right, and to put its competitors in the wrong. Some critics of the *Rose* have proceeded by assuming some speakers to be privileged over others. Following Cerquiglini's lead, I prefer to regard JdM's text as a compilation, or montage, of different subject positions all held in play.

Furthermore, the various speakers do not themselves command a single, clear-cut perspective. I have already spoken of the ironic way each undercuts his or her own position: Raison talks of folly, Ami of friendlessness, Nature gestures towards the

supernatural, and so on. The 'narrator' figure is no safe guide here
either. Although distinguishable from the 'lover' in a general way,
the distinction is not rigorous or clearcut. The rubricators who have
identified 'L'Amant' and 'L'Aucteur' in the margins do not always
agree which comes where (*37*, pp.94-95). The sagacious cleric
participates in the folly of the lover: indeed, he eggs him on. And
the clerical first person is hard to pin down. It is less a historical
individual than a whole tradition of clerical culture: not a person
who speaks, but the works of Juvenal, Theophrastus, Virgil, and the
rest. This zeal for quotation is shared by several of the
personifications, notably the Ami, and the Ami's fictional character,
the Vilain Jalous.

A theme common to all of them, for which reference to earlier
writers is most consistently made, is antifeminism. Antifeminist
discourse has a long history in the Middle Ages and surfaces in very
similar forms in texts from different centuries and in different
languages (see *18 passim*; *30*, pp.20-23; *50*, pp.48-86, esp. 62-63).
Thus for example the Vilain Jalous bolsters his anti-marriage
argument with an appeal to the authority of Valerius, who appears
in the court satire of the twelfth-century Latin writer Walter Map,
and who is only the most recent link in a chain of quotation
stretching back through St Jerome to Theophrastus:

> n'est nulz qui mariés se sente,
> s'il n'est fox, qu'il ne s'en repente.
> Prode fame, par saint Denis!
> dont il est mainz que de fenis,
> si cum Valerius tesmoigne,
> ne puet nul amer qu'el ne poigne
> de granz poors et de granz cures
> et d'autres mescheances dures. *   (8685-92 [8655-62])

The narrator himself acknowledges this weight of tradition behind

---

* 'There isn't anyone who doesn't repent when he experiences marriage,
unless he's a fool. By St Denis, the worthy woman (rarer than a phoenix as
Valerius bears witness), no one can love her without her searing him with
great fears and anxieties and other cruel misfortunes.'

his writing. In a much-quoted passage, he hopes that women will not take offence at what they read since the content derives from earlier writers:

> D'autre part, dames honorables,
> s'il vous semble que je di fables,
> por menteor ne m'en tenés,
> mes as actors vous en prenés
> qui es lor livres ont escrites
> les paroles que j'en ai dites
> et celes que je en diré;
> que ja de riens n'en mentiré,
> ne li prodomme n'en mentirent
> qui les livres anciens firent.
> Et tuit a ma raison s'acordent,
> quant les meurs feminins recordent...[*]
>   (15215-26 [15185-96])

It is not the 'author' speaking, but *all* authors, with their combined *author*ity. The first person of such writing is not an individual but a tradition which, because it is passed by one learned text to another, I shall call an 'intertext'. At times the 'I' of JdM's narrator, and of his personifications, is thus an intertext, sustained by collusion between men against women, and hence strongly marked for gender.

The subject position in GdL is contained within the traditional discourse of lyricism, which promotes male subjectivity whilst also permitting courtship. Subjectivity in JdM is less simple. It is associated with bodily desire (in the case of the lover and women under the influence of Venus) but (in the case of literate men) it is also diffused through a clerical, and frequently misogynistic, intertext. The importance of this first person which speaks from

---

[*] 'Moreover, honourable ladies, if you think what I say is fictitious, don't regard me as a liar, but hold the authors responsible who have written in their books the things which I have said and will say. For I shan't lie, nor did the upright men who wrote those ancient books lie. And they all agree with me, when they record women's character...'

between books confirms what Cerquiglini has identified as the
writerly character of the *dit*. This brings me to the final section of
this chapter, in which I shall consider how far the first person in the
two parts of the *Rose* depends on the existence of writing.

(iii) Writing

The entire *Romance of the Rose* is an example of what Huot
has called lyrico-narrative composition (*37*, p.1 onwards), in that it
has, as it were, one foot in the oral, performed discourse of the lyric,
the other in the writerly and readerly discourse of romance. The
lyric element is, as I have argued, particularly strong in GdL's part
of the romance. But orality is also an important feature of the work
of JdM, whose lover is given to outbursts of feeling, and whose text
is peopled by speakers communicating orally with listeners. Several
of their speeches, indeed, belong in essentially oral genres such as
the lecture (la Vielle), or the confession (Nature). These are all
forms defined by the use of the spoken medium and by the physical
presence of speaker and listener.

The writerly element, though more to the fore in JdM, is
however also important in GdL. As noted above (p.44), an
important preliminary act of the first-person protagonist is to read
the images on the outer side of the garden wall and choose to pass
beyond them. The crucial visit to the Fontainne d'Amors confronts
him with a narrative of the life of Narcissus, adapted from Ovid,
and commemorated, according to 1435-38 [1433-36], in a stone
inscription. The first-person voice in GdL is a voice; it laments and
pleads; but it is also a written text, fixed in the writerly form of
octosyllabic couplets, unaccompanied by music, recorded so that it
may be read. It is an example of what Huot calls performative
writing, preserving and transposing to the written medium the
features that characterise sung lyric.

In JdM writing is no longer something to be alluded to
sporadically but an insistent condition. His own text, as we have just
seen, has been partially generated by the writings which preceded it,
the misogynistic tradition which he does no more than pass on.
Genius, Nature's chaplain, reads out a sermon from a written script

(19483 [19453], 19492 [19462]) instructing man to undertake various forms of sexual 'work' ('ploughing', 'hammering' etc.), including 'writing': man should recreate himself by 'writing', with his 'pen', on the 'tablets' provided by Nature (see 19545 [19515], 19629-36 [19599-606], 19673-76, [19643-46] etc.). These images themselves come from a written source: Alan of Lille's *Plaint of Nature* (*8*, e.g. pp.134, 156; and cf. *44*, pp.72-76). The written, then, serves as an image of continuity both in culture (we rewrite the books of the past) and in bodily existence (we 'write' children for the future). And, Genius's sermon assures us, such 'writing' will secure our eventual entry to paradise: commenting on the Fontainne d'Amors scene in GdL, Genius criticises it and proposes an emended text which invokes not earthly, but heavenly, prospects (see Chapter 5, pp.84-93; on Genius as a writer, see *20*, pp.120-28). If men 'write' properly, they will gain entry to this textual paradise...

Whereas GdL 'fixes' oral performance in a written text, JdL uses the written text to compare bodily impulse with clerical inspiration and scandalously offers, from their conjunction, a place in heaven for the good writer – or for the energetic 'writer'. As a compiler, JdM assembles disparate elements which jostle together in the kind of montage described by Cerquiglini as typical of the *dit*. The first person lurches unpredictably between outrageously jarring discourses. GdL's narrative, although written, still observes the control and decorum of court performance. Writing in JdM sheds these inhibitions and licenses new kinds of play, which will be explored in the next three chapters.

4. Narrative Play

The next three chapters all revolve around the notion of play in the *Romance of the Rose*. By 'play', here and at the end of the preceding chapter, I do not primarily mean 'gamelike quality', though neither do I intend to exclude this meaning entirely: JdM is certainly a playful writer, and GdL's elegantly ironic rituals can be seen as a kind of courtly game. I mean, rather, play in the sense of space for movement; instability; uncertainty: as one might speak, for example, of 'the play in a machine' or 'the play in a system'. Such movement, or play, is evident in JdM. But it already characterises GdL's *Rose*, and may help to explain JdM's alleged love for it (10584 [10554]).

(i) Repetition and chronology

This play arises in part because of the text's lack of commitment to narrative. Although continuing to refer to the *Rose* as a romance, I have already argued that it has much in common with the more meditative, and static, genres of the lyric and the *dit*. In 4000 lines Guillaume de Lorris does not tell much of a story. The first-person subject enters the garden, sees the rose, falls in love with it, kisses it once, is repulsed, and finds further advance blocked by Jalousie's construction of a castle round the rose bed. For anyone who has experienced the rapid pace of Marie de France's *Lais* or of *La Mort le roi Artu*, this will seem decidedly slow going. JdM's rambling manner is, at times, a still greater test of patience. True he finishes the 'story': the quest for the rose is fulfilled. But it takes him 17000 lines; and he proceeds, essentially, by recapitulating events from GdL: encounters with Raison, Ami, and Amor, interview with Bel Acuel, fresh imprisonment of Bel Acuel, reappearance of Venus. In other words, apart from the dénouement, Jean's text is less action than re-enactment: the interest lies not so much in narrative as in reworking earlier material.

JdM's rehearsal of his predecessor's narrative incidents is far from innocent. Systematical shifts of detail and emphasis undermine GdL's courtly decorum. In his hands, the intellectual and moral stature of the lover declines (cf. above, p.42). The Ami who advises him in JdM is full of ingenious suggestions about how to seduce and retain a woman. Deceit and bribery (or 'present-giving') form the basis of seduction (7307-7986 [7277-956]). To keep a woman once she has been won, the trick is, apparently, to avoid outright confrontations over infidelities on either side, and to swear whatever she wants to hear; any difficulties can readily be smoothed over by frequent sexual intercourse (9689-852 [9659-822]). Such cynicism is a worrying revision of Ami's counsel in GdL that the lover should placate Dangier in order to gain closer access to the rose. When, subsequently, Fausemblant offers to help Amor, and sets out with Contrainte Abstinence to murder Malebouche, we are left to infer that hypocrisy and violence are the best supports the lover can turn to. The amplified roles of the Vielle and Venus present us with a view of feminine sensuality far removed from the courtly restraint of GdL. Love, it appears, has left the idyllic world of the court romance for the seamy, and steamy, milieu of the fabliaux, where idealism is less an irrelevance than a downright handicap. Lewis was surely wrong, then, to blame these repetitions of his predecessor's plot on JdM's lack of narrative invention (*48*, p.140): the shift to a different ethical climate is pervasive and strategic.

This play can, in fact, be read as a response to a dominant narrative device of earlier romance: that of cyclical repetition. In Chrétien's romances, events keep part-repeating themselves, and such repetitions often seem to convey a thematic seriousness. In *Yvain*, to take an obvious example, the hero, banished for having slighted his wife, becomes locked in an obsessive pattern whereby he assists women who, for a bizarre array of juridical and fantastical reasons, find themselves in difficulties. This compulsion to repeat a secular gesture is, in itself, a reworking of the clerical trope of *contrapasso*, a spiritual narrative in which the individual is able, through successive re-enactments, to eliminate past errors and so come closer to perfection. The implication, both in the clerical use of *contrapasso*, and in its adaptation by humanist romancers of the twelfth century (such as Chrétien), is that repetition brings improvement. Since JdM's redeployment of GdL's plot, on the contrary, brings a consistent drift away from moral ideals, his version of the *Rose* can be read as a parodic rejection of such ethical optimism.

There is already a good deal of repetition in GdL. Many of the scenes of his part of the romance, like successive stanzas of a lyric, elaborate different aspects of the love-experience, rather than marshalling them along a narrative thread. When the dreamer looks into the Fontainne d'Amors, he has a presentiment of love. This 'stanza' (1571-1614 [1569-1612]) is about apprehension at the madness and danger of love, to which Narcissus's death bears witness. The dreamer then sees the rose garden reflected in the crystals, and the mood changes to rapt admiration at the beauty and youth of the desired rosebud (1615-80 [1613-78]). Next follows a lengthy description of the god of love firing five arrows at him (1681-1880 [1679-1878]): the first two, Biauté and Simplece, pierce his eye, and the remainder, Cortoisie, Compaignie and Biau Semblant, his heart. Each arrow produces a fresh burst of suffering, and the point of the sequence seems to be to generate lyric intensity rather than to contribute to a narrative. Considered in context, these 'arrows' replicate and elaborate the love which has already been inspired by the sight of the rose; considered in themselves, they represent less a sequence than a cycle, since the last (Biau Semblant) is an enhanced repetition of the first (Biauté). Amor then takes the dreamer prisoner, praises his courtly qualities, and accepts his homage:

> Atant devins ses hons mains jointes,
> et sachiez que mout me fis cointes
> dont sa bouche baissa la moie:

ce fu ce dont j'oi graignor joie. *

(1955-58 [1953-56])

This is another 'lyric' development in which erotic fascination with
the lady is blurred with submission to the abstract principle of love,
a submission imaged by the ritual of feudalism. The scene goes on
with Amor locking the lover's heart with a golden key. This
presumably signifies that it belongs henceforth to Amor and not to
the dreamer, and so is a replication, using a different metaphor, of
the feudal image, in which the vassal's joined hands, placed within
the hands of the overlord, grant the latter control over his vassal's
person. This part of the romance concludes with Amor's instructing
the dreamer in the ways of love (to 2764 [2748]). We have worked
through 1000 lines for very little in the way of narrative advance.
Figurative and literal chronology do not correspond; a single,
engulfing experience ('falling in love') is being diffused through a
series of lyric stanza-like moments, each realised as a kind of
tableau.

A similar principle of diffusion operates on the literal level of
GdL's text. There are, for example, too many roses: in chaplets
worn by the dancers in Deduit's carole, on Amor's robe; the
dreamer wants to have a chaplet of flowers himself, and the rose
garden is full of roses. There are, as well, too many desirable
women, and too many couples. The text is shot through with
references to the paradisal qualities of the garden, so that when we
meet the 'god' of love and he issues ten 'commandments', the
religiosity of these terms has been fully anticipated. Such insistence
on a small vocabulary of key images is typical of dreams. So is the
reiterated sensation of encountering obstacles in one's path: the
garden wall, the hedge around the rose garden, Jalousie's castle.
Altogether, these features undermine the sense of narrative

---

* 'Thereupon I became his vassal, and did homage with hands pressed
together, and I can tell you that I was most gratified that his mouth kissed
mine, and this was what gave me the greatest joy.'

progression: the apparent 'story' dissolves into obsessively recurring images of the dreamer's desire and its frustration.

The treatment of narrative by the two authors of the *Rose* confirms the observations of the previous chapter. Whereas GdL's text is too 'lyrical' to be wholeheartedly 'narrative', too concerned with sentiment to develop a storyline as its main interest, JdM's continuation is more a kind of commentary on narrative, or 'metanarrative', a conclusion which accords well with Cerquiglini's account of the *dit* as 'meta-écriture'. Whereas GdL's use of repetition tends to 'fill' the text with idealised sentiment, JdM's tends on the contrary to 'empty' it of idealised anything. The play in chronology of GdL reproduces the obsessive intensity of dream-logic, enhancing the value of desire; the narrative play in JdM erodes our commitment to elevated emotional or ethical 'realities'.

(ii) Mise en abyme, framing and digression

The chronological opacity of GdL can also be illustrated by considering Amor's long speech to the lover, which forms the central section of his part of the text and contains much of the gist of it translated into non-figurative form.

In the course of this speech, Amor tells the dreamer of the sufferings of lovers, and gives as an example the fact that when they go to bed at night, their sleep is troubled by dreams of the beloved (2423-46 [2411-2434]). The dreamer thus has a dream in which what he dreams informs him that he will dream what he is already dreaming about. There is a possibility of infinite recursion here: he dreams that someone tells him that he will dream that someone tells him that he will dream... the pattern could go on for ever. The term *mise en abyme* is often used to refer to this self-mirroring pattern.

Amor's whole speech functions as a *mise en abyme* of the surrounding allegory. He starts by telling the dreamer the ten commandments of love: avoid rusticity, never slander others, be wise and courteous, eschew obscenity, don't be arrogant, dress elegantly and keep yourself clean, be joyous, brave and generous. These instructions replicate and 'explain' the figures on the garden wall and in Deduit's dance. The dreamer, by entering the garden, has already rejected the elements excluded from it – uncourtliness, felony (identified by Amor as the chief fault of the slanderer, 2096 [2084]), poverty and avarice; he has, since his admission by Oiseuse, been associated with joy, pleasure, courtliness, generosity, and so on. Thus the 'ten commandments' are less a narrative advance than a rehearsal, in literal terms, of the allegorical configurations through which the lover has already passed. (Admittedly there is no personification corresponding to commandment nine, be a brave knight, though there are Arthurian knights in Deduit's dance.)

Amor's speech also rehearses in literal terms some of the developments which follow it. After dreaming of your beloved, he says, the lover should go to her house and hope that she will hear his lamentations:

> Et se la belle sans plus veille,
> ce te lo je bien et conseille
> qu'el t'oie plaindre et doloser,
> si qu'el sache que reposer
> ne pues en lit por s'amitié.
> Bien doit fame aucune pitié
> avoir de celi qui endure
> tel mal por li, se trop n'est dure. *
>
> (2527-34 [2513-20])

Such instructions announce, and to some degree explain, the interactions between the dreamer, Bel Acuel and Dangier which follow this scene. This exchange between the literal and allegorical could go on indefinitely, with one being translated into the other and back again, an infinite number of times. The form which this *mise en abyme* takes is benign, since we gain an impression of reciprocal confirmation between the authority of Amor's speech and the validity of the surrounding narrative. His speech is framed by

---

* 'And if the lovely one is awake, I advise you to ensure that she overhears your grieving and laments, so that she knows that you are unable to rest in your bed for love of her. A woman should feel some pity for a man who endures so much suffering for her, unless she is excessively hard-hearted.'

the episodes either side of it; but since it also explicates them, we could also see it as providing the framework which gives them meaning.

JdM follows GdL in that he uses many devices of framing, but differs from him in that the overall effect is far from reassuring. The structure of his continuation could be represented as follows:

Raison	Nature, Genius
Ami	Vielle
Amor and Fausemblant	

That is, the alliance between Amor and Fausemblant is framed twice: once by Ami and the Vielle, speaking for male and female sexual experience respectively; and once by Raison and the Nature-Genius duo, all theorists of the human condition, with Raison hostile to Amor and the other two prepared to assist him. If GdL provides instruction on how to read the romance at its centre, so, in a sense, does JdM; but the advice is of a very different character. Fausemblant's warning against credulity is worth quoting from again (cf. above, pp.28-29):

> Sanz faille, traïtre sui gié
> et por traïtre m'a Diex jugié.
> Parjur sui, mes ce que j'afin
> set l'en envis jusqu'en la fin;
> car plusor por moi mort reçurent
> qui mon barat onc n'aperçurent,
> et reçoivent et recevront
> que ja [més] ne l'apercevront.
> Qui l'apercevra, cis iert sage;
> gar s'en, ou c'iert son grant domage.

> Mes tant est fort la decevance
> que trop est grief l'apercevance... *
> (11169-80 [11139-50])

This warning is salutary, given the complexity of the double frame surrounding him. The philosophising of Raison and Nature-Genius contrasts with the murky pragmatism of Ami and the Vielle, but all their speeches overlap and contradict one another in this ironic play of perspectives, so it is vital to recall that the structure of the whole text is a kind of double parenthesis around the message 'don't be taken in!' (Not all readers of the *Rose* would be alert to precise details of this structure, perhaps; yet the overall effect of balance in the poem is unmistakable.)

Fausemblant's perturbing instruction is echoed by the example of *mise en abyme* in Nature's speech. This is the passage (discussed pp.16-18) dismissing erotic dreams as illusory, and quoting as an example something remarkably like the *Romance of the Rose*. GdL's dream-character Amor sets up a recursive pattern which is self-confirming ('love makes you dream of love makes you dream of love...'), even though he acknowledges that you may be disappointed on waking. But Nature's account of dreams implies an infinite regression into unreliability ('dreams delude you that you are being deluded that you are being deluded...').

The analysis of the structure of JdM's continuation which I gave above is not the only possible one. It implies that the speeches by the various personifications are the major events of the text, and reduces the plot to the status of infil. In fact the opposite analysis is made by Lewis: according priority to the story, he categorises the speeches as 'digressions' (*48*, p.138 ff.). Either way of reading JdM

---

* 'There is no doubt that I am a traitor, and God has condemned me as treacherous. I am a perjuror, but my ends are impossible for anyone to know until the end; for many have died because of me, who never perceived my trickery, and they go on receiving death, and will continue to do so, without ever perceiving it. If anyone does perceive it, he will be a wise man; let him be on his guard against it, or suffer the consequence. But the deception it [my trickery] involves is so great that perception of it is extremely difficult.'

is possible: we can see the speeches as parentheses within the action, or the action as parentheses between the speeches. It isn't easy to decide what is 'central' and what 'marginal' or 'digressive'. Picking out the main structure of the continuation is subject to uncertainty or 'play'.

The speeches also raise the issue of what is the frame, and what is framed. They are plainly 'digressive' in their tendency to wander from the point; I have already said a little about this in Chapter 2, pp.31-32. A classic form of digression occurs when the speaker diverges from a particular subject for a while, and then returns to it. This sets up a loop within the speech which is enclosed by the surrounding matter. In some cases several loops are embedded one within the other. Ami's speech, a particularly elaborate example of successive looping, is represented by Poirion (*66*, p.125) in the following diagram:

beginning	theme	ending
7333 [7303]	lying and hypocrisy	9894 [9864]
7887 [7857]	covetousness	9679 [9649]
8355 [8325]	Golden Age	9526 [9496]
8455 [8425]	jealous husband	9492 [9462]
8561 [8531]	Lucretia, Heloise	8832 [8802]

As Poirion shows, the beginnings and endings of particular loops are carefully signalled. Clearly this organisation is highly sophisticated. It is the antithesis of narrative, in its constant return upon itself; and it produces an interesting play of meaning between the different levels or loops. In particular it makes one query the category 'digression'. Is the material within the loops a digression, and thus something one can discard? Or on the contrary, is it being set off as central, major importance being conferred upon it by the care with which it is framed? I shall illustrate the play between these two ways of constructing JdM's writing with some examples of my own.

Raison's speech sets up a loop between lines 4377-88 [4347-58] (definition of *amor*, a quotation from the famous treatise on love composed by Andreas Capellanus at around the turn of the twelfth and thirteenth centuries) and lines 4590-4602 [4560-72] (definition of *bon'amor* in opposition to *amor*). Here are the two passages which demarcate the loop:

Amors, se bien sui apensee,
c'est maladie de pensee
entre deus persones anexes,
franches entr'eus, de divers sexes,
venans as gens par ardor nee,
par avision desordonee,
por eus acoler et baisier
et por eus charnelment aisier.
Amors autre chose n'entent,
ains s'art et delite et entent.
De fruit avoir ne fait il force,
en deliter sans plus s'efforce. *   (4377-88 [4347-58])

Mes de la fole amor se gardent
dont li cuer esprennent et ardent
et soit l'amor sans convoitise
qui les faus [cuers] de prendre atise.
Bon amor doit de fin cuer nestre,
dont n'en doivent pas estre mestre
nes que font corporel soulas.
Mes l'amor qui te tient ou las
charnel desir te represente,
si que tu n'as aillors entente. **   (4593-4602 [4563-72])

---

* 'Love, if I reflect properly, is a disease of the mind between two individuals in close proximity, freely interacting and of different sex, which comes born of the desire, as a result of excessive feasting of the eye, to kiss and embrace and give each other sensual relief. Love has no other aim; all it does is burn, delight and desire. It doesn't care about bearing fruit, but strives after pleasure and nothing else.'

** 'But they should guard against that foolish love which makes their hearts

The similarities of diction between these two passages (*ardre /
esprendre / atiser*; *entendre*; *charnel / corporel*; *aisier / deliter /
soulas*), and their joint condemnation of love, prepare for and mark
off the material between them, whose theme is that the proper
purpose of coupling is procreation, not the search for pleasure
(Delit). This theme is most emphatically formulated in two more
parallel passages which form the frame to a further loop: 4422-28
[4392-98] and 4557-62 [4527-32]. The material in between derives
from Cicero's *De Senectute*, and is an exposé on the dangers of
youth.

   These successive loops seem to be classic digressions in that
they stray further and further from Raison's apparent theme: the
superiority of *bon'amor* over *amor*. But they also serve indirectly to
undermine GdL's part of the *Rose*. The allegorical figure of Delit
can be seen as Raison's answer to GdL's Deduit; whereas Deduit is
presented in a positive light, Delit is quasi-diabolical, his name
suggesting 'crime' as well as 'delight'. The attack on youth,
similarly, can be read as a riposte to the celebration of Jonece, and
exclusion of Viellece, in GdL. Thus it could be maintained that it is
inside the loops that the argument with GdL's notion of Amor is
most effectively, if surreptitiously, conducted. What is framed is in
fact what provides the polemical framework of Raison's entire
speech: a demolition of the ideology of Amor as she discerns it.

   The instability between 'digression' and 'centrality' often
serves, however, to undermine a speaker's own case. On three
occasions, Raison offers herself to the lover as the one true object of
love (vv. 5842-50 [5812-20], 6371-81 [6341-51], 6872-74 [6842-
44]). Each of the loops set up between these passages contains
prolonged descriptions of Fortune and admonitory historical
examples (*exempla*) of the sufferings of her victims. Here Raison
dwells at length on what she is trying to ward off. Like others of

---

catch fire and burn, and their love should be without the cupidity which
incites false hearts to acquisitiveness. Good love should be born of a true
heart, and they should not be governed [by material things], any more than
by bodily solaces. But the love which holds you in its snare represents
carnal desire to you, so that you have no mind to anything else.'

JdM's figures, Raison gives greater prominence to what she denounces than to what she recommends.

The play between frame and framed is particularly noteworthy in the long speeches by Ami and the Vielle. Both refer to the myth of the Golden Age: a kind of Classical equivalent of Eden, before the fall of man, when there was freedom and abundance on the earth. (The main source of the Golden Age myth is Ovid, *Metamorphoses* I; it was extensively elaborated and commented upon in the Middle Ages: see *52*, pp.144-48; *34*, pp.417-24; *77*, pp.272-74.) In each case the myth is part of a looping structure, but in diametrically different ways. In Ami's speech, the myth is divided into two parallel passages which frame the intervention by the Vilain Jalous:

> Encor n'i avoit roi ne prince
> meffais, qui l'autrui tout et pince.
> Tretuit pareil estre soloient,
> ne rienz propre avoir ne voloient.
> Bien savoient ceste parole,
> qui n'est ne mençonge ne fole,
> qu'onques amors et seignorie
> ne s'entrefirent compaignie,
> ne ne demorerent ensemble:
> cis qui mestrie les dessemble. * (8445-54 [8435-44])

> Mes li premier, dont je vous conte,
> ne savoient que nagier monte.
> Tretout trovoient en lor terre
> quanque lor sembloit bon a querre.
> Riche estoient tuit ygaument
> et s'entramoient loiaument.
> [Ausinc pesiblement vivoient,

---

* 'No king nor prince had yet resorted to crime, taking and stealing other people's property. All were accustomed to being equal, with no desire for personal property. They knew well the truth of this saying, which is neither deceitful nor foolish, that love and lordship never kept company or could abide together. Whoever assumes mastery drives them apart.'

car naturelment s'entramoient,]
les simples genz de bonne vie.
Lors ert amors sanz seignorie,
l'un ne demandoit rienz a l'autre. *
                    (9517-27 [9487-97])

Between these two passages the Vilain Jalous rants against his wife
in particular, and women in general, for their constantly threatened
and uncontrollable infidelities. In the Vielle's speech, instead of the
theme of marital jealousy being inserted into the Golden Age theme,
it is the other way round. (For a rather different intepretation of
ironic framing in this speech, see *33*.) She has been talking about
the way women pretend to be jealous in order to exert pressure on
their husbands (13823-39 [13793-809]); she then goes on to recount
the jealousy of Vulcan, husband of Venus (13840-74 [13810-44]);
then comes the Golden Age passage celebrating an idyll of sexual
freedom (13875-14158 [13845-14128]); then a return to the story of
Vulcan (14159-98 [14129-68]); and finally a return to the theme of
women pretending to be jealous, the better to control their husbands
(14199-226 [14168-96]).

We might read these loops in two ways. In Ami's speech, the
fact that the Golden Age forms a frame around the Vilain Jalous's
desire for mastery could be seen as containing and condemning his
behaviour; in the Vielle's, the framing role is given to 'real-life'
sexual behaviour, and we might be led to conclude that the Golden
Age is now only a memory, or a myth, well beyond the reach of
contemporary sexual-political experience. Yet the 'digression' (or
content of the frame) can also be read in each case as undermining
the frame. Thus in Ami's speech, we might feel that the Golden Age
is being relegated to 'fantasy' by the 'reality' of the Husband's

---

* 'But the first men, of whom I tell you, had no sense of the value of
navigation because they found in their own land everything which seemed
desirable to them. They were all equally rich/powerful, and loved one
another loyally. They were a straightforward people, with virtuous lives,
who lived together in peace because they loved one another in accordance
with nature. In those days there was no lordship in love, and no one asked
anything of anyone else.'

conjugal difficulties (although these in turn are undermined by further loops; cf. *50*, pp.75-76); and in the Vielle's speech, that the myth can provide a rallying point, and a rationale, for women's discontent with their sexual predicament. (I return to the Vielle's lecture on pp.103-04, 105, 106-07.) Either speech on its own raises a problem of what is central, and what is marginal. Taken in conjunction, they illustrate JdM's perverse and playful refusal to commit himself to any unambiguous position. The loops in his text, which make up the major part of it, mark a refusal to narrate along a simple linear path.

(iii) Disorder and dissemination

In GdL, as we saw, certain motifs – roses, women, couples, thoughts of paradise, barriers – keep recurring. These repetitions, I suggested, give his text the kind of dream-like insistence which will be familiar to any dreamer. They may not belong in 'realistic' narrative, but they impart a certain psychological coherence to his writing. JdM picks up this obsessive quality, which I imagine was very attractive to him. He keeps reproducing fragments and reminiscences of GdL's garden across his own text. These reminiscences appear to be quite random but often the context suggests a new light on their meaning.

An example occurs in Ami's use of the Golden Age myth. This time 'des premiers peres / et de nos premerainnes meres' (8355-56 [8325-26]) offered an abundance of fruit, eternal spring with daily birdsong (8407-10 [8377-80]), and everyone, 'puceles et valez proisiez' went round decked in flowers and dancing (8419-20 [8389-90]), 8439 [8409]). GdL's description of the garden in the opening lines of the romance has made an unexpected return. The aristocratic paradise garden now appears as a state before culture began, before agriculture, government or crime: a time without property or lordship, when love was guiltless and constantly on tap. Depending on how we apprehend Ami's use of the Golden Age, we might infer from this that GdL's garden is a product of nostalgia for a pre-symbolic state of innocence; or else that it is pure pie in the sky, a fantasy which has no place in the political realities of modern life. Another shifty recycling of GdL's text occurs in the speech by JdM's Richece. The lover asks for admission to the path of Trop Donner, but she refuses: only her intimates are allowed to 'quaroler, dancier et baler' (10086 [10056]), crowned with garlands of flowers (10102 [10072]), in the meadows, gardens and woods where young men and ladies are joined together by 'vielles maquerelles' (10095-96 [10065-66]). Here money and prostitution have penetrated GdL's fantasy, and corrupted it. A final, fleeting instance of this narrative dissemination is Raison's description of the house of Fortune, which not only picks up the allusion to Fortune's wheel in GdL (3981ff. [3953ff.]) but also, with its contrast between the placid waters on one side, and the turbid, dangerous ones on the other (5980ff. [5950ff.]), recalls the dual nature of GdL's Fontainne d'Amors, whose waters are at once enticing and perilous. This general tendency to dwarf or marginalise GdL's garden has been further described by Smith (*70*, pp.230-38).

It is not only GdL's text which is dismembered and flung around in this way by JdM. He is just as happy to do it with his own material. The best instance of this is, in fact, a story of dismembering and throwing: the myth of the castration of Saturn and birth of Venus has as its narrative content the fragmentation and scattering to which it is itself subject.

The myth is first introduced by Raison as part of her discussion of the sovereignty of *bon 'amor* over justice:

> Justice qui jadis regnoit
> au temps que Saturnus vivoit,
> cui Jupiter copa les coilles
> son fis, cum ce fussent andoilles,
> puis les geta dedens la mer,
> (mout ot ci dur filz et amer)
> dont Venus la deesse issi... *   (5535-54 [5505-11])

---

* 'Justice, which used to reign at the time when Saturn was alive, whose testicles Jupiter, his son, cut off as though they were sausages and threw into the sea (what a harsh and bitter son) from which the goddess Venus emerged...'

The story of the castration of Saturn and birth of Venus is an origins myth, marking the end of a reign of Justice and the beginning of the disorderly times in which we now live (see *42*).

Elements of this passage are disseminated throughout JdM's continuation. For example, there is a comic proliferation of other origins myths, several of which share the theme of seeds being dispersed and coming up in another guise, just as Saturn's genitals are thrown away and return in the form of Venus. Nature recounts the myth of Deucalion and Pirra who repopulated the earth after a flood by obeying an oracular instruction to throw the bones of their mother over their shoulder. They interpret this as meaning that their mother is the earth and her bones its rocks. From the stones thrown by Deucalion men are born, and women are produced by those thrown by his wife (17598-650 [17568-620]). Dispersal gives rise to metamorphosis, and the metaphorical mother, the earth, becomes a literal one when her 'bones' (an image of death) are transformed into life. Likewise Cadmus, Genius tells us (19736-50 [19706-20]), sowed dragon's teeth, which sprang up as armed knights; but unlike the 'children' of the Deucalion myth these proceed to kill each other down to the last five, who then assist in the founding of Thebes. Here dissemination, as in the Venus narrative, begets violence and disorder; the reader who knows anything of the history of Thebes will be aware that conflict extends long after its foundation, characterising the stories of Oedipus, Eteocles and Polynices, and beyond. Genius concludes the Cadmus story on a complacent tone:

> Mout fist Cadmus bonne semence,
> qui son peuple ensi li avence.
> Se vous ensi bien commenciés,
> vos linages mout avanciés. *   (19749-52 [19719-22])

But the moral which he draws – that men should take heart from Cadmus's experience and procreate – sorts oddly with the myth, which rather suggests that procreation, a further sowing of seed, is as likely to beget death as to thwart it.

---

* 'Cadmus sowed a good seed; in this way he furthers his race. If you begin well like that, you further your lineage greatly.'

These origins myths involve conflicting accounts of unpredictable and potentially violent transformations. The drift of meaning – bones to stones to people, teeth to knights to corpses to procreation – is more suggestive of movement round in a circle than of a clearly delimited point of origin. In this light, the 'sowing' of fragments of GdL's *Rose* and their re-emergence in transformed and disorderly forms suggests not the consciously controlled refashioning of a determinate model, but a drift into constantly shifting meanings.

Venus, the byproduct of Raison's telling of the castration of Saturn, is to become a major figure of disorder and transformation in the text. It is she who brings consummation for Pygmalion, a miracle she will repeat for the lover by bringing Jalousie's castle down in flames and so giving him access to the rose. Between the mention of her by Raison and the dénouement, she figures occurrently, both as a participant, and in narratives told by the other figures. Her fragmented biography is scattered across the text, with no regard to its chronology. We have already seen how the Vielle frames her telling of the Golden Age myth with an account of how Venus deceived her husband Vulcan; Venus's infidelities with Mars are also discussed by Nature and Genius (18061-129 [18031-99]). Between these two passages, the narrator tells at length the story of Adonis (15675-764 [15645-734]), whom Venus loves *after* she has tired of Mars. Adonis is, however, a descendent of Pygmalion; so his birth is first mentioned at the very end of the text, long after he has died!

The Venus story, then, is part of the fall-out of the myth of Saturn's castration. As well as being told out of order, it is also a narrative of disorder. Venus breaks down marriage and paternity, the fabric of patriarchal society. Amor mentions her love affairs, so innumerable that none of her children know who their father is (10833-34 [10803-04]). He himself has a grave distrust of his mother (10749-56 [10719-26]), and would prefer to win the rose for the lover without her interference – but that proves impossible. Venus is determined not to allow Chastity to subsist in any living woman (15830-34 [15800-04]), and her power alone is irresistible.

The myth of Saturn will be alluded to on many occasions in the *Rose*, either directly, or through references to other castrations (such as those of Abelard, 8796 [8766]; and Origen, 17052-53 [17022-23]). But the most elaborate retelling of it occurs in Genius's sermon (20032-60 [20002-30]). In depriving Saturn of his testicles, Genius maintains, Jupiter was worse than a murderer, because he inflicted loss on Saturn's girlfriends (!), prevented his having progeny, and perverted his moral character. It is in Genius's account that the end of the Age of Gold is most explicitly treated 'allegorically', in terms of Christian theology, since it becomes identified with the Fall from Eden (see *34*, p.418; *42*). Before it, man was 'whole' and lived in peace and plenitude; after it, he is diminished, condemned to struggle and labour. But although Genius allegorises, he is also painfully literal-minded, since according to him, the means of restoring man to his state before the Fall is by successful erection, penetration and insemination (cf. *44*). Through energetic sexual work ('ploughing', 'hammering' and above all 'writing'), salvation, he assures his listeners, will be theirs. Although Saturn has been castrated to produce her, Venus, by providing ample opportunity for copulation, thus has a quasi-redemptive role: she restores the male genitals to their reproductive function. Saturn's castration is symbolically reversed: this origins myth goes round in a circle too. And dissemination has got right out of hand, as sexual and theological meanings hurtle scandalously against one another.

Improbable as this may seem, it was Raison who set these meanings on their collision course, and this is the last element in the dissemination of the Saturn myth that I shall discuss here. Raison's use of the word *coilles* (5537 [5507]) to refer to Saturn's genitals provokes a prudish outcry from the lover. Her response is to claim that names are merely conventional terms for things, and that we are behaving mistakenly if we associate with the name a reaction which properly belongs only to the thing it designates; furthermore, we should not permit ourselves to condemn things which form part of God's creation, since He made them good. She supports this claim with a practical example: if relics were called 'testicles' we would worship them; if testicles were called 'relics', we would protest that it was a dirty word (7106-7122 [7076-92]). In fact it is neither the word, nor the thing, but *acoustumance* ('social conditioning', 7137 [7107]) which governs our reactions, and pushes us to devise endless euphemisms; we would be better advised to speak openly.

Raison is here proposing yet another origins story: she is the inventor of language, who has identified 'things' and assigned them 'names'. In her view, 'relics' and 'testicles' are totally different things, and their names are cited because of their independence of each other. Our reaction as readers, and the remainder of the text, show the deficiencies of this theory. As Poirion has put it in a very thoughtful article, 'derrière le mot, le doute atteint la parole' (*67*, p.9): not only are the notions of the genital and the sacred now irremediably (and comically) associated with one another, but any mention of the sacred which could possibly be attracted into the orbit of obscene meaning is so instantly. The sustained image of the 'pilgrim' with his 'staff' approaching the 'reliquary' and so bringing the dream to its conclusion is only the most obvious example of this. The meaning of words, far from being safely lodged in 'things', swirls off in the same uncontrollable way as the meanings of stories.

In GdL, the absence of narrative coherence leads to the text being suffused with a subdued and dreamlike eroticism, which gives it a compensating coherence of a different kind; exchanges between the 'literal' and 'allegorical', mediated by Amor's central speech, confirm this thematic cohesion. In JdM, by contrast, narrative is much more riotous. It challenges the conventions of romance, and frustrates the reader's attempts to sort out the main lines of its development from potential digressions. The diffusions operated in GdL's text are replaced by dissemination, the scattering or drift of meaning, a major emblem of which is the story of the casting away of Saturn's seed and its return as the goddess Venus.

Such a text is clearly resistant to systematic interpretation. There are, however, two general points I should like to make before closing this chapter. JdM's continuation has been referred to as an encyclopedia of existing knowledge (e.g. *60*, pp.341-46). JdM was, indeed, contemporary with the encyclopedist Brunetto Latini; the thirteenth century saw a proliferation of didactic compendia in the vernacular as well as in Latin. The use of personifications gives a misleading impression that JdM might, indeed, be doing the same: a reader wanting to find out about 'Nature', for example, might think of looking up the section of the work in which she speaks. I think it is more helpful, however, to see his continuation as an anti-encyclopedia. As an archive of knowledge, the *Romance of the Rose* is useless because it has no user-friendly retrieval system. The dissemination of the myth of the Age of Gold is a telling example: there is no principle according to which this topic is classified. On the contrary, it turns up in different forms all over the place. The story of Venus is presented with maximum incoherence. Similarly it is impossible to guess that 'the Trinity' is filed under 'Nature' or 'Nero' under Raison. Philosophical issues are scattered here and there (*59*, p.52). If you want to find something in this text you actually have to read it; that is not what a compendium is for.

My second point is that whilst JdM foments disorder of all sorts, there is a clash which seems to gratify him particularly: that of sexual and religious meanings. This has been the feature of the *Rose* which has attracted most critical attention, from the Middle Ages to the present. It will be approached from two different points of view in my next two chapters.

5. Imaginary Play

This chapter considers the clash between sexual and religious meanings in terms of the relationship, in the *Rose*, between the mind and the body. The body – specifically the faculty of sight – is important for three aspects of the poem. First, the love quest for the rose begins when the dreamer sees it. Second, the *Rose* is, in the broadest sense, an educational text. It purports to instruct its readers and offers them a fellow pupil within the text, since the dreamer is the recipient of a great deal of advice and information (*31*, p.50); parts of the poem are specifically concerned with visual perception as a means to acquire knowledge. Third, the fact that the *Rose* is a dream vision means that the visual is central to its literary technique. The title *Miroër as amoureus*, assigned to the work by JdM, epitomises this three-way combination with its mention of lovers, its allusion to the pedagogical tradition of *Specula* or *Miroirs*, and its evocation of the analogy, in medieval thought, between a mirror and a text.

In all these three aspects, however, the role played by the physical sense is only a partial one. Love strikes through the eyes; but it affects the heart and mind as well; and it can be portrayed as a spiritual experience. This interrelation of the physical and the mental was systematised in the medieval notion of the degrees of love (or *gradus amoris*), according to which love begins with sight, and advances gradually towards other forms of interaction; the relevance of this schema to the *Rose* has been explored by Calin (*21*, p.118). Similarly, if information can be conveyed through the senses, reasoning and spiritual revelation are also important means to knowledge. And while a dream-vision poem appeals to the visual imagination of its audience, it does so through the medium of a verbal discourse which also includes narrative and exposition, and may lay claim to visionary inspiration.

In both parts of the romance, the quest for love and the quest for knowledge go hand in hand. Each of these two themes centres on a desiring self, whether its object be sex or enlightenment; and so both themes also conduce to some investigation of this self. Since the mind and the body are where love and knowledge are to be located, this investigation focuses particularly on the relation between the physical and mental or spiritual aspects of human nature. Towards the end of the romance, this relation is increasingly defined as a tension between body and soul.

The study of these complex issues is necessarily limited here (but see also *43*). I shall examine in turn the status of the visual imagery in the *Rose*; the role of the mirror of Narcissus in relation to love, knowledge, and the production of the text; and finally Genius's sermon. More explicitly than previously, this sermon orchestrates erotic quest, the theme of knowledge (as revelation), and the theme of writing, in a wild speculation about human nature. A major source of play in the *Rose* is, I shall argue, the uncertainty about the capacity of the image to convey useful or truthful information.

(i) *Visual perception and the visual image*

The modern term 'dream vision' implies the extent to which medieval allegorical poems in the tradition of the *Rose* invoke the sense of sight. Manuscripts of the poem respond to its pictorial character with often profuse illuminations (see *46*). These have been studied by, amongst others, John Fleming, whose approach relies on the belief that images are a readable alternative to linguistic exposition (*28*, p.12; and cf. *74*, pp.3-55). The impulse to the pictorial in GdL is constant: his text is less a 'narrative' (as we have seen) than an unfolding of *tableaux* and *tableaux mouvants*. Its use of personification starts with the painted images on the garden wall, and continues with lengthy descriptions of the appearance of Oiseuse and Deduit's dancers. GdL does not explicitly discuss the interpretation of images, but there is an implicit recommendation to read his text as if it were visual. Pictures and description are equated, most obviously in the account of the images on the wall, but also in descriptions of the dancers: Deduit is so beautiful that 'he resembled a painting' (812 [810]), Leesce's nose is so perfect that 'you couldn't make a better one in wax' (850 [848]).

Yet images and text are not equivalent. Pictures contain a wealth of material; and they present it all at once, unlike language, whose content can only be presented in one dimension, along the linear chain of utterance. This difference is elaborated in one of JdM's sources: the *Anticlaudianus* by Alan of Lille. Painting, Alan says, is comparable with the philosophy of Plato, which offers 'inspired visions of the secrets of heaven and earth... and tries to search the mind of God' (7, p.49). Text, by contrast, resembles the philosophy of Aristotle, with its emphasis on the subtleties of logic. Alan follows Plato's lead, and gives preference to painting: 'Thus this art's power subtly checks logic's arguments and triumphs over logic's sophisms' (ibid.). In this passage he is discussing an actual painting: a mural. He later makes the same claim for embroidery, saying of the robe worn by the *puella poli*: 'What the tongue cannot tell the picture does: how language, since it fails to reach the essence of God, grows senseless when it tries to express things divine, loses its power of communicating and tries to take refuge in its own meaning' (7, p.141). For the Latin neo-platonist poets of the twelfth century, the lack of equivalence between text and image is interpreted in favour of the image. They try to make their texts more like pictures (though not to the extent of abandoning writing for visual art, of course: Alan's claims are, to that extent, self-undermining). The superiority of images provides part of the rationale for writing dream vision poetry whose major theme is that of 'intellectual pilgrimage from the sensible world to the level of vision and theology' (78, p.90).

A less sanguine view of visual representation than those of either GdL or Alan is found in JdM. He relies more on speeches than on description to characterise his personifications, and although appeal to the visual is obvious in occasional set pieces such as the House of Fortune (5920-6174 [5890-6144]), or the bringing of Venus from Cytheron in her dove-drawn chariot (15659-800 [15629-770]), these passages are borrowings from earlier texts.

Rather than claiming the superiority of art to language, JdM stresses its inadequacy to nature. Art kneels before Nature (16020 [15990]), eagerly inquiring her secrets. Although Old French *art* may mean any craft (*59*, pp.45-46), the visual arts predominate in this passage:

> Car Art, cum [bien] qu'ele se pene,
> par grant estuide, par grant pene,
> de faire choses quex que soient,
> [...]
> toutes herbes, toutes floretes
> que valeton et puceletes
> vont en printemps es gaus coillir,
> que florir voient et foillir,
> oisiaus privés, bestes domeches,
> baleries, dances ou treches
> de beles dames bien parees,
> bien portretes, bien figurees,
> soit en metal, en fust, en cire,
> ou quelcunques autre matire,
> soit en tabliaus, ou en parois,
> tenans biaus bachelers as dois,
> bien figurés et bien portrais,
> ja por figure ne por trais
> ne les fera par eus aler,
> vivre, movoir, sentir, parler. *
>   (16035-37, 16049-64 [16005-07, 16019-34])

Art's failures to represent natural phenomena are here enumerated apparently at random, but gradually work round to include another

---

* 'For Art, however much she strives with great industry and effort to make anything whatever, [...] all the green plants and flowers that young men and girls go to gather in the woods in springtime, and which they see flowering and coming into leaf; tamed birds, domesticated animals; dances of all kinds by lovely ladies in fine clothes, well drawn or modelled in metal, wood or wax or any other material, in pictures or on walls, holding handsome young men by the hand, likewise well modelled and drawn, [however much she strives] she will never, whatever the modelling or drawing, succeed in making them go on their own, live, move, feel or talk.'

instance of what I have called (pp.65-66) the 'dissemination' of GdL's text. The implication is that if art in general is deficient, that of GdL is so in particular: depictions, in whatever medium, of beautiful dancers in a garden, are woefully inadequate.

But if GdL is vulnerable to criticism, so too is his continuator. The way JdM develops this passage acknowledges good-humouredly the inadequacy of visual representation in his own text. For he has reached a point where a description of Nature is called for (and where, in the corresponding place in his source for this part of the romance, Alan's *Plaint of Nature*, there is a highly elaborate one extending over several books, *8*, pp.73-112). For 80 lines (16165-248 [16135-218]) which comically exaggerate the traditional 'ineffability topos', JdM protests not only his own inability to produce an adequate portrait of Nature's beauty, but the impossibility of the task for even the greatest painters, sculptors and writers. God who made her would alone be competent. Humorously underlining the inadequacy of language for description, JdM ends this 'digression' with an utterly banal courtly portrait:

> ... tant est avenant et bele
> que flor de liz en may novele,
> rose sus rain, ne noif sor branche
> n'est si vermeille ne si blanche. *
>
>   (16241-44 [16211-14])

The similes of flowers and snow recall several of GdL's portraits: cf. 545-47 [543-45], 804-05 [802-03], 840-41 [838-39], 1193 [1191]. In thus emphasising the deficiencies of art, JdM, influenced here by thirteenth-century aristotelianism (*59*, p.47), marks his disagreement with the neo-platonist Alan of Lille, and mocks both the poetic efforts of the first author of the *Rose* and his own.

The theme of sense perception and interpretation reappears in JdM's continuation within the discourse of Nature herself (*26*, p.94). She recommends the study of Aristotle ('who noted the things

---

* '... [her face] is so attractive and lovely that a fresh lily flower in May, a rose on its stem or snow on bough, is not so scarlet or white.'

of nature better than anyone since Cain', 18032-33 [18002-03]) as a means to understanding the formation of the rainbow, and then urges the study of the Arab scholar Alhazem's work on optics in order not to be fooled by optical illusions. Mirrors in particular need to be studied before their images can be made use of (18044-196 [18014-166]); but diseases of the eye, as Aristotle ('who knows well about this matter', 18198 [18168]) testifies, also distort visual perception; and the eye is subject to all sorts of optical illusion (18209 ff. [18179 ff.]); the ignorant think this is the work of demons. Nature goes on from here to talk about the delusions of the inner eye of the imagination, gradually working round to the fantasies produced in dreams (especially dreams such as that described in the first part of the *Rose*). Very shortly after this point, Nature makes the comparison between kings and paintings, both of which look better from a distance (18570-78 [18540-48]). In discussing that passage earlier (p.44), I suggested that it reflected on GdL as a reader of images. Nature, then, keeps implicitly criticising GdL's unanalysed reliance on the visual. Bodily sensations, or imaginings, should not be read naïvely. They have to be interpreted in the light of science, which goes beyond surface data to discern the latent regularities of the material world.

The problems attached to reading the visual, and especially the visual arts, are thus a recurring theme in JdM; and one that can consistently be linked with the problem of reading poetry. For Alan of Lille, the lack of equivalence between painting and language was to painting's credit. For JdM, however, the problem of the image is that it has to be read as though it were a text: it needs to be made sense of. It therefore presents, in an aggravated form, the problem of allegory generally: that it both provokes, and resists, interpretation. Visual impressions need to be subjected to rational investigation – the body needs the mind to understand it. But Nature, creator of all things physical, is superior to all the efforts of the human mind, and so, although we may learn something from the visual representations of art, they will never be other than defective.

(ii) Image and mirror image: the role of Narcissus

Sight first becomes an important theme in GdL in the Narcissus episode, which was one of the most widely illustrated in the manuscript tradition of the poem (*28*, p.93). Wandering away from Deduit's dance, the dreamer comes to the Fontainne d'Amor. The Narcissus story is recalled. The dreamer then looks into the spring and sees the rose reflected in it. Shortly afterwards, the first two of Amor's arrows strike him through the eye. The grounding of love in sight has been established.

The Narcissus story is of course itself not only a story of love excited through the eyes, but of love for a reflection. This is how GdL recounts the latter part of it:

> Et quant il vint a la fontainne
> que li pins de ses rains covroit,
> il se pensa que il bevroit;
> sus la fontaine tout adens
> se mist lors por boire dedens;
> si vit en l'iaue pure et nete
> son vis, son nés et sa bouchete,
> et cis maintenant s'esbahi,
> car ses ombres l'ot si trahi,
> qui cuida veoir la feture
> d'un enfant bel a desmesure.
> Lors se sot bien Amors vengier
> du grant orgueil et du dangier
> que Narcisus li ot mené.
> Bien li fu lors guerredonné,
> qu'il musa tant a la fontainne
> qu'il ama son umbre demainne,
> si en fu mors a la parclose... *   (1478-95 [1476-93])

---

* 'And when he came to the spring that was shaded by the branches of the pine tree he thought that he would lie face downwards to drink from the spring; and in the pure, sparkling water he saw his face, nose and dainty mouth, and was taken off guard, for his reflection deceived him into thinking that he saw there the form of a wonderfully beautiful child. Then

Narcissus makes the error of loving what he takes to be another but is in fact himself. His eyes have misled him, or rather, he has been unable to interpret their evidence. His fatal misrecognition of his own reflection can be read as indicating Narcissus's inability either fully to recognise the self, or to see beyond it. Thus the mirror simultaneously prevents reciprocation (since Narcissus loves only himself) and blocks narrative, since the 'love plot' simply doubles back on itself, in the stasis of the mirror-image.

This looping back on itself of the Narcissus story anticipates the reader's sense of it as a digression. The dreamer's experience appears to take a quite different form from that of Narcissus: he doesn't see his own image, instead he sees the two halves of the garden, each reflected in one of two crystals in the water of the spring; and from this panorama he selects the single rosebud which is to obsess him for the remainder of the poem. Thus whereas Narcissus loved himself and became a flower, the dreamer loves a flower which is emphatically other to himself (cf. above, pp.45-46).

Nevertheless, as with other 'digressions', the Narcissus story has perhaps more relevance to the text than first appears. The dreamer himself stresses the resemblance between the perils of the mirror for him and for Narcissus (e.g. 1571-94 [1569-92]). Love is to bring him close to extinction, even if he has made a wiser choice of object than Narcissus did. Besides, as I have already argued, the 'otherness' of the rose is in some ways a delusion, since the dreamer's object of desire is assimilated back to the self, through the figure of Bel Acuel, who seems to be a double of the lover (see p.46, above). So whereas Narcissus loves himself in the guise of another, the dreamer loves another in the guise of himself. Both figures are constrained by the homosocial pressures which make only masculine qualities desirable; they can only love projections of the masculine self. That is, there is an inevitable component of narcissism (in the popular sense) in their desire. The mirror

---

Amor was well able to take revenge for the pride and the rebuff which Narcissus had dealt him. He got his due reward, for he gaped so long at the spring that he fell in love with his very own reflection, and in the end he died...'

constrains not only the destiny, but also the object-choice, of the men who look into it.

The image of the beloved, produced by the mirror of Narcissus, is not the only element in the story which undoes the apparently firm demarcation between self and object. All the images in the text are the products of the subjectivity of the dreamer, but are misidentified by him as being 'other people'. For example, he doesn't recognise Raison as being his reason, or Amor as his love. Similarly, the whole fabric of the dream is presented as an objectively 'real' landscape, not perceived as emanating from himself even though it is a production of his fantasy.

It is helpful, then, to see the Fontainne d'Amor as a 'fountain of allegory', that is, as a clue to the functioning not only of the theme of love, but of the wider mechanisms of the text. David Hult develops this idea (*36*, pp.263-300), drawing attention to the process of enlightenment in this scene, that is, to the importance of juxtaposing ignorance ('then') with improved perception ('now'). The very fact of repeating the Narcissus story provides an instance of this double perception since we ('now') know what Narcissus failed ('then') to apprehend, that the image which he loved was himself: cf. 1483-88 [1481-86], cited above. A similar transformation of perception is conveyed by the lapse of time between the dreamer's experience at the fountain and his composing the poem:

> Mes de fort hore m'i miré.
> Las! tant en ai puis soupiré!
> Cis mirëors m'a deceü:
> se j'eüsse avant cognëu
> quex sa force ert et sa vertus,
> ne m'i fusse ja embatus,
> car mentenant ou las chaï
> qui maint homme a pris et trahi. *   (1607-14 [1605-12])

---

* 'But a dreadful hour it was for me that I gazed into it. Alas! How much have I sighed since! This mirror has deceived me: had I known earlier what were its strength and its power I should not have approached it, for immediately I fell into the snare which has caught and betrayed many.'

In this connection, Hult points out the complex way in which the crystals are described as functioning (*36*, pp.277-79). We are explicitly told that there are two of them, each reflecting one half of the garden:

> Ou fons de la fontainne aval
> avoit deus pierres de cristal;
> [...]
> tout l'estre du vergier accusent
> a ceus qui dedens l'iaue musent;
> car touz jors, quel que part qu'il soient,
> grant partie du vergier voient;
> et s'il se tornent, maintenant
> pueent veoir le remanant. *
>
> > (1537-38, 1561-66 [1535-36, 1559-64])

And yet between the two parts of this quotation, there is only one crystal in the manuscript followed by Lecoy:

> quant li solaus, qui tot aguiete,
> ses rais en la fontaine giete
> et la clarté aval descent,
> lors perent colors plus de cent
> ou cristal, qui par le soleil
> devient inde, jaune et vermeil.
> Si est cil cristaus merveilleus... **   (*2*, 1541-47)

Hult suggests that rather than a scribal error we have here a differentiation between the crystals (plural) referring to the two stones at the bottom of the spring, and the single, crystal-like mirror of the water. This double vision, he proposes, represents 'the

---

* 'At the bottom of the spring there were two crystals; [...] they display the whole layout of the garden to those who stare into the water; for wherever they are they can always see a great part of the garden; and if they turn, they can see the rest of it straight away.'

** '... when the sun that watches over everything casts its beams into the spring and its brightness descends downwards, then more than a hundred colours appear in the crystal which, because of the sun, becomes deep blue, yellow and scarlet. The crystal is so wondrous...'

renewed perception afforded by the Fountain. The filter, or faculty of perception, and not the object perceived, is the central concern' (*36*, p.286). Such double vision is at the very root of allegory which offers both an immediate and a subsequent reading.

A different account of the role of the mirror in GdL's allegory has been put forward by the Lacanian critic Jean-Charles Huchet. He too starts off from the fact that there are two crystals. The garden is never visible as a totality, only as two halves. For Huchet, this line of fracture serves to mark the simultaneity of the 'imaginary' and the 'symbolic'. (The term 'imaginary' in Lacanian psychoanalysis designates a way of – erroneously – believing that we can construct quasi-pictorial representations of ourselves as solid, whole and entire; it is opposed to the symbolic, which recognises the contingency, linearity, and partiality of the constructions of the self by language.) The mirror of the crystals invites the self to conceive of itself as whole and ideal (an 'imaginary' self); but the fact that the image is fractured serves as a reminder of the lack which is inherent in symbolic representation (*35*, p.169). In Lacan's thought, this lack arises when the child accepts the dictates of social existence, and agrees to participate in language; to do so, he must sacrifice the desires which are not sanctioned by the social order and which therefore become literally unsayable or unthinkable. The entry into language is thus a traumatic event involving unspeakable loss and condemning the subject to unsatisfiable desire. For Huchet, this explains why the rose is such a poignant love-object: it cannot be attained because it is only a rose, and all that it can tell us is that desire is, by its very nature, incapable of fulfilment (*35*, pp.171-77). At the same time, the subject's exposure to such desire comes about as a result of his accepting the social domination of language. The Fontainne d'Amor is surrounded by personifications which represent words as live powers affecting the lover's career, and which are thus an enactment of the symbolic order that defines and constrains him.

We have seen, then, that the fountain scene in GdL serves several functions. It initiates the dreamer to love through the eyes in a context which makes us reflect on the relation between love for the self and love for another. And it also serves as a parable of perception, using different images, or perspectives, as a means to enlightenment. It may further, if we follow Huchet's suggestions, offer a commentary on the relation between desire and language, an issue of importance in both GdL's text and modern psychoanalytic thought. Thus although GdL does not speculate theoretically on the relation between image and text, an important episode of his romance offers an interesting commentary on both the themes and the form of his romance.

Before proceeding to a consideration of how JdM reacts to all this we need to include one more aspect of this scene: the fact that the fountain has a traditional place in representations of paradise gardens (cf. *69*, p.36 ff.). Described by the dreamer himself as a *paradis terestre* (e.g. 636 [634]), the garden in the first part of the *Rose* is presented in quasi-religious terms. Like many love poets before him, GdL uses the language of spiritual experience to describe experiences whose founding moments, at least, are grounded in the senses. This gives a particularly emphatic turn to the issues at stake in this chapter. Is the depiction of the garden of love as a paradise to be interpreted as a statement about love or about paradise or both? Is the 'spiritual' being used as an 'image' of the 'sensual' or the other way round, or do the terms remain somehow separate, despite their formal juxtaposition in the dream vision? Furthermore, depending on how we respond to these questions, what are the implications of such imagery for our conception of the relation between the senses (here: sight) and the mind or soul? Does the equation of a sensory garden with a range of religious concepts (paradise, angels, ten commandments, God of Love) involve commitment to some kind of continuity between mind and body, and if so, how?

Such questions are surely very far from GdL's mind as he reproduces the courtly religiosity familiar from the troubadours (e.g. Bernart de Ventadorn) or Chrétien (in the *Charrete*). But they provoke strong reactions in JdM, as we shall see. In his text, the relation of the fountain of Narcissus not only to love, but to understanding, knowledge and religion, becomes paramount.

(iii) Image, imagination and 'imaginary' in Genius's sermon

Genius is one of the most problematic figures in JdM's *Rose*. His role has already been discussed in connection with the theme of writing (pp.50-51) and the conjunction of sacred and sexual meanings in the Golden Age myth (p.69). Those ideas will now be developed and drawn together through a consideration of Genius's commentary on GdL's fountain scene. I shall start by placing this commentary in the sermon as a whole.

Anathematising all who fail to collaborate in reproduction, and inciting his listeners to obtain a plenary pardon by engaging in sexual 'work' (19694-95 [19664-65]), Genius contrasts the pains of hell with the pastoral enchantments of the 'parc du champ joli' (19935 [19905]) where ewes are led by the son of the Virgin (19938-39 [19908-09]). This park is immune to economic pressure. Flowers once grazed on spring up again (19979 [19949]); sheepskins are never sold nor meat eaten (19985 [19955], 19990 [19960]) and the shepherd never exploits his flock (19997 [19967]). The eternal brightness of this park is comparable only with the eternal daylight of Saturn's reign: and so Genius 'digresses' to tell the effects of Saturn's castration. Under Jupiter, people are subject to the random dictates of pleasure; property is instituted and men are condemned to labour and violence. They are enslaved, like black sheep who have no will to follow the path of the beautiful lamb, and let him turn their fleeces white (20209-16 [20179-86]). The mention of white sheep closes the loop around the Golden Age 'digression' and returns us to the description of the park. The 'beautiful lamb' is now identified (20243-20256 [20213-26]) with the shepherd of the earlier account. 'Lords,' says Genius, 'this lamb awaits you' (20267 [20237]). Now the comparison between his park and GdL's garden, which hitherto has only been implicit, becomes explicit as Genius condemns the rival garden:

> Car, qui du biau jardin quarré...
> a ce biau parc que je devise...
> fere en vodroit comparoison,

il feroit trop grant mesproison,
s'il ne la fait tel ou semblable
cum il feroit de voir a fable. *
   (20279, 20283, 20285-88 [20249, 20253, 20255-58])

For the next 300 lines Genius pores over GdL's text, concentrating
especially on the scene at the fountain:

C'est la fontainne perilleuse
tant amere et tant venimeuse
qu'el tua le bel Narcisus
quant il se miroit par dessus.
Il meïmes n'a pas vergoigne
de reconnoistre la besoigne,
et sa cruauté pas ne cele
quant perillous miroir l'apele
et dit que, quant il s'i mira,
maintes fois [puis] en soupira,
tant se trova grief et pesant.
Vez quel douçor en l'yaue sent!
Diex, cum bonne fontene et sade,
ou li sain deviennent malade!
Et cum il s'i fait bon virer
por soi dedens l'iaue mirer!
 Ele sort, ce dit, a granz ondes
par deus doiz creuses et parfondes;
mes el n'a pas, car bien le soi,
ses doiz ne ses yaues de soi;
n'est nulle chose qu'ele tiengne
qui tretout d'aillors ne li viengne.
Puis si redit que c'est sans fins
qu'ele est plus clere qu'argens fins.
Vez de quex trufes il vous plede!
Ains est [si] noire et troble et lede,

---

* 'For anyone who were to draw a comparison between the lovely square
garden and the lovely park that I describe would be greatly in error unless
he made it in terms of that between truth and fiction, or roughly so.'

> chascuns qui sa teste boute
> por soi mirer, il n'i voit goute. *
>
> (20409-20436 [20379-20406])

Genius goes on to contrast the fountain of Narcissus with the spring in the garden of the lamb which reveals the true nature of things. The waters of this spring are clear and the crystals are replaced by a carbuncle which simultaneously is round, and has three facets (an image of the Trinity). Perpetual light shines from this carbuncle, so that there is no night:

> Si ra si merveillous pooir
> que cil qui la vodrent vooir,
> si tost cum cele part se virent,
> [et] lor face en l'iaue remirent,
> touz jors, de quelque part qu'il soient,
> toutes les choses du parc voient,
> [et les congnoissent proprement,
> et eus meïmes ensement:]
> et puis que la se sont veü
> jamés ne seront deceü

---

* 'This is the perilous fountain, so bitter and so poisonous that it killed the beautiful Narcissus when he gazed into it. He himself [GdL] is not embarrassed to recognise the business, and he does not dissimulate its cruelty when he calls it a perilous mirror, and says that, when he looked into it, he was often to sigh as a result, so grievous and distressing did he find it. Just see what sweetness he feels in the water! God, what a lovely and gentle spring, which makes the healthy ill! How good it is for you to turn towards, so you may gaze into the water! He says that it wells up from two conduits which are deep and hollow; but it does not have these conduits nor its waters on its own account, I know, for everything comes to it from elsewhere. And then he goes on to say that it is endless,and brighter than purified silver. What rubbish he is serving up! On the contrary, it is so black and turbid and hideous that anyone who sticks his head in it to gaze into it, can't see a thing.'

(I have translated *soi mirer* as 'gaze into' rather than 'see oneself reflected in', though both meanings are possible. The implication of changing to the second of the two translations would be to emphasise the theme of self-knowledge, or its absence, over that of perception in general.)

> de nulle chose qui puisse estre,
> tant y deviennent sage et mestre. *
> (20567-78 [20537-48])

The sermon ends with Genius again inviting his listeners to choose between the two gardens, and urging them to 'serve Nature by labouring well' (20637-38 [20607-08]) in order to be able to drink from the true waters of the park.

A major part of this sermon, then, represents GdL's Fontainne d'Amor as a source of suffering, death, and deception. The enlightenment which GdL claims for it is rewritten as darkness, and a new source of eternal illumination proposed. The iconography of the rival garden, the *parc*, is recognisably Christian: the Lamb/Good Shepherd is Christ Himself, the virgin ewe His mother, and the white sheep the saved, while other aspects of the garden represent the Trinity, divine wisdom, eternal life, and other theological conceptions. The comparison between the two gardens seems straightforward: we are being asked to choose between earth and heaven. The Fontainne d'Amor offers nothing but the delusions of our mortal condition whereas the *parc* offers eternal life. The imagery of GdL is written off as sensual, Genius's own promoted as spiritual. The careful balance between physical love and moral enhancement which GdL's text aspires to is therefore rejected as a sinful illusion which could only lead to perdition.

Yet the 'orthodoxy' of this message is severely compromised. No Catholic preacher ever claimed that it was sex that got you into heaven (cf. *74*, pp.275-78). Genius's argument is that man will gain eternal life by serving Nature well, but the Christian notion of paradise offers salvation to the individual, whereas what sexual reproduction assures is the eternity (or rather, the perpetuity) of the species. Genius rides roughshod over Christian beliefs in the value

---

* 'And it has the further miraculous power that those who wish to see it, as soon as they turn in that direction and see their faces in the water, can always see, from wherever they are standing, all the things in the garden, and know them properly, and themselves too. And once they have seen themselves in it, they will never be deceived by anything there could ever be, they will be so wise and learned.'

of continence and virginity, regarding them as perversions, and threatening those who practise them with castration (19528-686 [19498-656], and see *59*, pp.162-64, *60*, pp.281-82). Venus and Amor clearly regard the whole episode as a great joke. They robe Genius as a bishop, setting him up like a figure from pantomime to deliver his sermon:

> Tantost li diex d'Amors afuble
> a Genius une chesuble;
> anel li baille et croce et mitre
> plus clere que cristal de vitre.
> [...]
> Venus, qui ne cessoit de rire
> ne ne se pooit tenir quoie,
> tant par estoit jolive et gaie,
> por plus enforcier l'anatheme
> quant il avra feni son theme,
> li met ou poing un ardant cierge
> qui n'estoit pas de cire vierge. *
>
> (19477-80, 19484-90 [19447-50, 19454-60])

Although he starts by invoking 'the authority of Nature' (19505 [19475]), Genius's pronouncements are as much 'authorised' by Venus and Amor, whose interests they directly serve. (Recall that at the end of the sermon the rose is finally won.) In short, the whole relation between sacred and sensual, mind and body, is far less simple than the comparison between the two gardens would suggest. Critical responses to the sermon, accordingly, vary enormously. Some see in it an admittedly comic celebration of natural fecundity (*63*, pp.202-03), others a denunciation of the idolatry of sensual lust (*28*, pp.223-26), yet others a synthesis between different but

---

* 'At once the god of Love dresses Genius up in a chasuble and gives him a ring, a bishop's staff and a mitre brighter than crystal from a window. [...] Venus, who couldn't stop laughing and wouldn't keep quiet, she was in such a jolly mood, sticks a burning candle in his hand, not made of virgin wax, in order to make the condemnation more forceful when he gets to the end of his address.'

analogous accounts of the relation between body and soul (*56*, pp.116-25).

Divergent as these responses are, they have in common a reluctance to allow the text to admit contradiction, resolving the opposition between the sexual and the sacred in one direction or the other, or else eliminating it in favour of 'synthesis'. (Another way out of the problem is by recourse to the notion of 'parody', cf. *62*, p.57.) I prefer to start by admitting that the contradictions really are there, and that they are not going to melt away in a few pages of critical writing – or even a few years of scholarly research. They are there, in my view, because this text seeks to challenge boundaries and principles of order, rather than reaffirm them. In earlier Latin tradition Genius had accumulated a multiplicity of associations which lead to his crossing the most important of those boundaries, that between mind and body, and the resulting confusion is what JdM sets out to exploit.

The word *genius* is related to the Latin word *ingenium* which can mean 'imagination' (*78*, pp.94-95). JdM perhaps acknowledges this etymological connection when he has Genius speak of the devices of the imagination, the *engin* (20179 [20149]) with which men try to limit the hardships of life in the reign of Jupiter. The figure of Genius himself can designate the faculty of imagination (*79*, pp.45, 56-61). As such, he spans mind and body, because the mental pictures in which imagination deals are formed in the mind, but rely on the visual sense. In twelfth-century thought, this combination can pull in two directions. Imaginings may be based in the senses, as when we call to mind sensory experiences; or they may figure spiritual realities which we have never, literally, seen, but which we can best represent to ourselves in pictorial form (*79*, pp.46-51). This two-way pull of imagination lends it to ironic investigation (*79*, p.50). It also, however, offers an account of allegorical writing. The capacity of a fable to contain a spiritual truth is analogous to the way the body imprisons within it the soul (*56*, pp.56-63). The figure of Genius in Alan of Lille's *Plaint of Nature*, who like JdM's Genius anathematises those who fail to follow Nature (though in a more serious vein than is the case in the

Rose), 'represents an archetypal poet-philosopher' (*56*, pp.60, 112).
This range of meanings of imagination parallels that of dreams (*56*,
pp.57-58, 107), and so links Genius with the genre of dream vision
poetry generally.

We have already seen that JdM is more sceptical than Alan of
Lille about the value of the pictorial imagination. In 'borrowing'
Genius from the twelfth-century neoplatonist tradition, then, he is
also citing the conception of writerly imagination held by twelfth-
century allegorists: primarily Alan of Lille, but others (such as
Bernardus Silvestris) as well. When he compares the two gardens,
JdM's Genius is attempting to relegate GdL's text to the 'lower'
kind of imagination, in which images relate to physical experience,
and to substitute a 'higher' allegory in which images construct
transcendent truths. GdL's 'enlightenment' is therefore Genius's
sensual delusion: the imagination of 'courtly love' is opposed to a
neo-platonic dream vision of spiritual realities. Unfortunately, as we
have seen, Genius has great difficulty establishing the superior
credentials of his proposed text. His use of twelfth-century neo-
platonism is only a citation, set off from the rest of his sermon by
invisible quotation marks, and vulnerable to being read ironically
(cf. *79*, p.60).

The reasons for this are of various kinds. The *parc* itself is a
somewhat trite affair. Even Gérard Paré, who writes as a
Dominican, finds the sheep imagery mawkish (he complains of
'mièvreries', *60*, p.287). But more important, the ambitions of neo-
platonist allegory are undermined by the tug of imagination towards
the sensual, as is shown by Genius's other forays into metaphor. In
the account of the *parc* the traditional character of the imagery
makes acceptable – indeed, imperceptible – to the reader the idea
that 'imagination' involves 'finding pictorial images of spiritual
ideas'. But Genius's other metaphors all direct us towards sensual
meanings. He dislikes the idea of literal ploughing, which is
included in the list of evil consequences of the reign of Jupiter
(20120 [20090]); but he recommends it as a metaphor for sex.
Genius's sexual metaphors suggest confinement of imagination to
the body. The recommendations to 'plough', 'write' and 'hammer'

are examples of obscene allegory, in that movements of the upper body (mainly the arm and hand) serve as euphemisms for those of the lower body. Instead of the pictorial imagination 'rising' to the spiritual it descends below the belt. If we see Genius as the figure of allegorical poetry, there is at least an irony, at most a fundamental contradiction, between the two different directions his allegory takes. His metaphor of Fall as castration and salvation as generation points to the gulf between the two poles of his 'imagination' far more than it reconciles them. His criticism of GdL, who likewise found paradisal qualities in his garden of love, is a case of pot calling kettle black.

Considered as a figure of writerly imagination, then, Genius contains the opposing poles of mind and body; but so far from being reconciled or 'synthesised', they pull against each other. The *parc* sequence in his sermon, however, also represents him as a reader; his discussion of GdL uses two quite distinct techniques. In proposing an alternative garden as a place of illumination, health and eternal life, Genius acts, indeed, as a poet. But in reinterpreting GdL's garden as a place of darkness, sickness and confusion, he figures instead as a reader and commentator, and an extremely powerful one. Genius can take GdL's allegory and assign to it meanings which are the reverse of the ostensible text. (Again, JdM may have in mind the allegorisations of non-Christian poetry by such twelfth-century readers as Bernardus Silvestris.) If we bear in mind the association between Genius and allegory, and take heart from his example, we have no reason to respect the letter of his text (cf. *44*).

To comment on Genius as he commented on GdL, it is helpful to bring in further associations of his name on which the text might be drawing. According to Nitzsche, Genius in twelfth-century thought presides over the descent of the soul into the body, which is necessary to the formation of the individual. The combination of soul and body is full of appetites and desires, which are also identified as its 'Genius'. Such desires may tend towards good (rationality) or evil (sensuality) (*56*, pp.41-66). One of their functions is to ensure the perpetuation of the species. For this reason, Genius may be particularly closely identified with sexual desire and with the genitals (*56*, p.90).

Now a figure who is both genitals and the soul is hard to make sense of. If we follow the downward tug, and read him as primarily sexual, then his whole sermon becomes an entertaining exercise in enlightened self-interest. A figure who represents the genitals would, after all, be bound to see castration as equivalent to perdition, and sexual reproduction as 'heavenly'! GdL's garden, which offers a prolonged and frustrating courtship, with no assurance of eventual consummation, would indeed strike him as a deceitful illusion, a source of death and despair. No wonder that he condemns it. On the other hand, if we grant Genius's spiritual credentials, we have to read his words in an equally radical way in the other direction. The sexual element in his sermon then becomes a metaphor of man's spiritual health. (It is used in a similar way in Alan of Lille, though more explicitly linked to other evidence of man's fallen state.) The proper exercise of our natural propensities becomes the means to heavenly grace, since if we can reflect Nature, Nature in turn is the reflection in the true mirror: that of God:

> Cist est salus de cors et d'ame,
> c'est li biaus mirooirs ma dame. *
> (19899-900 [19869-70])

Genius as allegory *might* be the route to perfect understanding since he shows us how to ground our knowledge in that which perfectly reflects divinity. The mirror of GdL brings only perils, this one has true perception.

As I said, a figure who is both genitals and the soul is hard to make sense of, and JdM seems more concerned to let the nonsense ride. The impossibility of deciding how to make the various parts of the sermon cohere together is part of the play. That is why, I think, the points of transition in Genius's argument are so extremely weak: it is baffling, rather than persuasive, to have eternal life equated with perpetuation of the species, and to have major argumentative

---

* 'He [God in heaven] is salvation of body and mind; He is my mistress's beautiful mirror.'

developments hinge on chance comparisons. If we look briefly again at Genius's commentary on the fountain scene, psychoanalysis serves here as in GdL to illumine the mechanisms of the text. A major theme of Genius's attack on GdL's garden is its lack of fixity, and its fragmentation; notably the fact that one can only ever see half the garden in the crystals. His own paradisal imagery expresses an aspiration to wholeness and plenitude; and this corresponds to the way in which, for Lacan, religion is another form taken by the imaginary since it offers fallen man the prospect of wholeness and completeness. But just as the imaginary in GdL is set beside a symbolic of restless desire that belies it, so in Genius's speech the imaginary paradise is contrasted with life lived in the shadow of castration, following the overthrow of Saturn by Jupiter. In the symbolic order, all thought is founded on the possibility of opposition which is epitomised by that between presence and absence, and identified, by Lacan, with the threatened loss (and thus absence) of the phallus. Without that founding opposition, we would be unable to institute contrary categories such as those of mind and body, or to seek to fix a boundary between them.

GdL does not represent the relation between text and image as a problem, but his use of the Fontainne d'Amor shows how visual reflections establish a causal link between sight and love, sight and knowledge; and this in turn initiates investigation of the relation between self and object, the literal and the allegorical. JdM, for whom the status of the visual was always problematic, reworks the same material in such a way as to create maximum confusion about the role of mind and body in sex and knowledge, and to license radical experiments in writing and commentary. So far I have framed the main point of my argument – that which concerns the relation of mind and body – as a problem of boundaries. But Genius's sermon is a scandal not only because it puts boundaries in question, but because boundaries define hierarchy. Mind and body are not just different domains: one is 'higher' than the other. Other, related, hierarchies are also destabilised by JdM's continuation. That is the subject of the next chapter.

6. Intellectual Play

This chapter will proceed in the opposite direction from previous ones: instead of first considering GdL, I shall continue the argument from the point reached at the end of the last chapter and return to GdL only after having discussed the play of thought in JdM's continuation. I have argued that the relation of mind to body was at issue in both parts of the *Rose*, and proposed that the courtly commonplaces of GdL are exploded by JdM. His continuation laughs at the paradox whereby sensual love is represented in spiritual terms, and draws attention to the divergence between sensual and religious language. I shall proceed in this chapter to show how this comedy affects the security of hierarchically ranked ideas, and how this in turn has an impact on political thinking in the *Rose*.

The question of the relation between mind and body was obsessively discussed by later twelfth-century thinkers, who explored hierarchical schemes on which to range the various faculties or levels of perception (*23*, pp.33-35, and more generally pp.159-90). Here is an example from *De unione corporis et spiritus* by the twelfth-century philosopher and theologian Hugh of St Victor. It is a commentary on John 3:6, cited by Wetherbee, *78*, p.61:

> Behold the ladder of Jacob. It rested on the earth and the top of it reached the heavens. The earth is the flesh, the heavens God. Our minds ascend in contemplation from the depths to the most high: from flesh to spirit through the mediation of the senses and sensory perception; from spirit to God through the mediation of contemplation and revelation.

This passage is looking to establish parallels between spiritual and physical realities, and then to map them, in a quasi-scientific manner, on to a progressive scale of perception. The ladder, with its contrast of 'high' and 'low' mediated by successive rungs, is the perfect image for this kind of hierarchy. Experiments with similar schemes, which flourished in the writings of Bernardus Silvestris and Alan of Lille, derive much of their inspiration from Boethius's *Consolation of Philosophy (9)*, which also presents a ladder-like progression from 'lower' to 'higher' truth. It is against this background of thought that this chapter examines JdM's *Rose*.

In the *Consolation*, Philosophy appears to the prisoner in a dream and sets about enlightening him. Much of the general pattern of her argument is reproduced by JdM (see *58, passim*). Towards the end of Book I, Philosophy consoles the dreamer by trying to persuade him that he should have no regard for Fortune, and she expands on this theme through books II and III. The gist of her teaching is resumed by Raison, JdM's first speaker. By Books IV and V of the Consolation, Philosophy is tackling more advanced subjects such as the relation between Providence and free will. Precisely this issue is taken up at length by JdM's Nature, well on in the continuation, who then goes on to talk about the mysteries of the Trinity, the incarnation, and such like – mysteries which, as she says, philosophers themselves cannot understand by reason. There is, then, in both texts an overall progression from seeing events from the perspective of man's reason alone (in which case their apparently random movements can best be explained by invoking 'Fortune') to understanding their place in a theological scheme in which both divine predestination and free will have their place.

In the systems of thought which take their cue from Boethius, the movement up the ladder of enlightenment is matched by progression up a ladder of faculties. Philosophers elaborate hierarchical schemes to show how different kinds of knowledge are apprehended by different faculties. Alan of Lille, for instance, discerns five of them: the senses, imagination, reason, intellect (with which we perceive spiritual beings) and intelligence (by which we know God) (*8*, p.30). In JdM, however, the upward movement is played off against a flagrantly provocative shift downwards, from the head (Raison) to the genitals, manifested first in their admittedly problematic representation as Genius, then in Venus (who embodies women's desire), and finally in the meeting of the dreamer with the rose (or, if we revert for a moment back to the upward hierarchy, of the pilgrim with the relics).

Thus JdM's continuation simultaneously obeys the Boethian tradition which works up a hierarchy of knowledge, and flouts it by working down the faculties of perception. This running of hierarchies against each other is the principle form of intellectual play in JdM, and the source of the major problems of interpretation of his work. (The twelfth-century neoplatonist works are far from straightforward in this regard. I am not claiming that JdM's play is specifically aimed at them.) The two movements, one up, the other down, intersect in the figure of Nature, whose speech contains striking conjunctions of the material with the spiritual.

(i) Nature

Unlike Alan's Nature, who lodges a complaint, JdM's Nature confesses – parodically, however, since the 'fault' is not hers – to Genius her priest (16285ff. [16255ff.]). Her initial apologies for her tears prompt Genius to a virulent tirade against women for faults from which he admits Nature is exempt (16314-706 [16284-676]), a speech referred to rather surprisingly as his 'comfort' of her (16708 [16677]). Nature has been represented as ceaselessly active at her forge, repairing the ravages of Death. In one of the finest passages in JdM's continuation, creation appears as a ferment of activity: Death chasing everywhere, catching anyone she can; individuals fleeing this way and that, trying desperately to avoid her clutches; and Nature, hammering away, producing new specimens so that however successful Death may be against individuals, she cannot put an end to species (15891-16016 [15861-986]). Nature starts her confession by describing her role as 'chamberlain' of God's creation (16772 [16742]). As such, she acts as God's chief official and deputy (*connestable et viquere*, 16782 [16752]). God devised the form, divisions and proportions of the universe, and entrusted their perpetuation to her. She watches over the 'beautiful golden chain that laces together the four elements' (16786-87 [16756-57]), i.e.

the whole interconnecting fabric of material creation; and
everything in it, except for one single creature, obeys her (16800
[16770]). Nature's role is thus presented in terms of twelfth-century
Christianised platonism (cf. *68*, pp.80-86): she is the material
reflection of God's spiritual intentions. So far, apart from the
parodic elements, she closely follows her model in Alan of Lille.

Nature then proceeds to work through the various parts of the
universe, eliminating from her 'confession' the parts that are
functioning as intended. In so doing, she is departing from the
Plaint to incorporate thirteenth-century Aristotelian-inspired
science, as taught at Paris University by such masters as Albert the
Great (*59*, pp.53-86). From the sky with the fixed stars (16801
[16771]) she quickly reaches the planets, whose movements detain
her for over 2,000 lines (16833-18966 [16803-18936]). Inserted into
this scientific treatise, however, is a protracted essay on why the
planets do not control our destinies. Nature argues that reason can
rise above and govern natural impulse (17087-100 [17057-70]).
Somewhat unexpectedly she continues:

> Mes de sodre la question
> comment predestination
> et la devine prescience,
> plene de toute porveance,
> puet estre o volenté delivre,
> fors est a genz laiz a decrivre. * (17101-06 [17071-76])

Imperceptibly Nature 'digresses' into theology. Free will is
compatible with God's foreknowledge, since God sees everything in
the presence of eternity whereas man's perceptions are all located in
time; man therefore has to work out the plot as he goes along,
whereas God knows the story already. This part of the 'confession',
as I indicated earlier, is based on Boethius's *Consolation*. Nature's
defence of free will leads her back to the subject of man's ability,
through reason, to dominate natural drives, but this time Nature also

---

* 'But the solution to the question of how predestination and divine
foreknowledge, full of every foresight, can exist alongside free will, is hard
to explain to laymen.'

includes reason's capacity to rise above accidents of fortune, and resist sin (17527-78 [17497-548]). If man can make sense of the movements of the stars, he can predict disasters and take preventive measures (17579-702 [17549-672]). And if he can thus manage his body, what can he not achieve with his soul, which is so much more powerful (17703-14 [17673-84])? Regretfully, in a whirl of thirteenth-century scholastic terminology (*espondre*, *opposer*, *respondre*), Nature admits that it would take too long to get to the bottom of these theological issues (17727-33 [17697-703]). But she stresses their relevance to her 'confession', since her 'enemy' might wish to plead innocence on the grounds that his conduct is God's fault not his (17774-76 [17734-36]). On the contrary, she maintains, his folly arises from a failure of self-knowledge, which is caused by failure to keep his reason clear, which stems from vice, which is the result of a failure to exercise free will, which she has just demonstrated him to possess (17862-74 [17832-44]).

But now Nature leaves theology: it is time to get back to talking about the skies (17880 [17850]). The second part of her scientific treatise deals with the weather, optics, and delusions, all of which were briefly discussed in the last chapter, and leads into the defence of clerks. She fears (18295-18303 [18265-73]) that she is being prolix, a characteristically female failing, but nonetheless devotes 600 more lines to this section. The planets at last dealt with, she dispatches with alacrity the elements (18967 [18937]), plants (18981 [18951]) and living creatures, reaching (at long last) the guilty party at line 19021 [18991]. Man alone, the pinnacle and epitome of created life, is worse than a wolf to her (19054 [19024]).

At this point, Nature again leaves the natural for the supernatural; the reasons for this are not clear at the time, and the transition is very abrupt. Admitting that she didn't make man's understanding, she contrasts her own works, which are material and temporary, with those of God, which are spiritual and enduring. Citing Plato with gusto, Nature celebrates the eternal soul. She then tells of what even Plato, as a pagan philosopher, couldn't understand: only a virgin womb could comprehend God and know the marvels of the Trinity (19119-45 [19089-115). Nature concedes that the virgin birth is beyond her comprehension (19161-62 [19131-33]), but this does not prevent her briefly expounding the incarnation, crucifixion and redemption. This excursus, it emerges, is an elaboration of the theme of man's sin: God having made man's reason, man used it to turn against Him, thus making necessary Christ's redemptive incarnation. Reminding us once more that women can't control their tongues (19218-20 [19188-90]), Nature at last gets to the nub of her confession: she repents that she ever made man and proceeds to enumerate his faults. He is proud, murderous, thieving, treacherous, envious, etc. (19225-34 [19195-204]) – a slave to all the vices. Evoking the pains of hell, she leaves it to God to punish him (19325 [19295]).

One fault, however, is Nature's particular concern: man's failure to do Amor's task with the 'tools' she has provided. This 'naturalism' again marks a divergence from the Nature of Alan of Lille, the emphasis of whose 'plaint' is ethical. So Nature concludes her 'confession' by sending Genius to Amor's camp to greet him and 'Venus my friend' (19343 [19313]), together with all the army apart from Fausemblant. Genius's message, committed to him by Nature, is to instruct them to multiply, on pain of excommunication:

> Dites li que la vous envoi
> por touz ceus escommenier
> qui vous vuelent contrarier,
> et pour assoudre les vaillans
> qui de bon cuer sont travaillans
> as regles droitement ensivre
> qui son escrites en mon livre,
> et forment a ce s'estudient
> que lor linages monteplient
> et qui pensent de bien amer,
> car touz les doi amis clamer. * (19378-88 [19348-58])

---

* 'Tell him (Amor) that I send you to excommunicate all those who seek to obstruct you and to absolve the worthy who labour away with a brave heart to follow the rules properly that are written in my book, and who greatly devote their minds to increasing their descent, and who are set on loving well, for all such people I call my friends.'

We saw in the last chapter Genius's somewhat free reworking of this message.

Nature's confession, then, is put together like a layer cake: alternating layers of 'science' and 'theology', with an icing of neo-platonism on top, and supported, as on a firm base, on the requirement to reproduce. As in Genius's 'sermon', the parodic character of the confession, with its frequent misogynistic asides, draws attention to the bizarreness of the whole concoction. And, like Genius, Nature has found admirers and detractors among *Rose* critics. My own preference goes to the view that different discourses regarding nature are being thrown into relief, in a sceptical response to twelfth-century models. This is the view of Lucie Polak, who argues that JdM's Nature makes for herself the most spiritualising claims of twelfth-century neo-platonism, whilst in fact occupying the most material and 'naturalistic' ground made available by thirteenth-century Aristotelianism (*68*, pp.90-93, 96-98). This refusal to synthesise conflicting philosophical traditions finds a parallel in Genius's sermon, as discussed in the last chapter.

But Nature's speech differs from that of Genius in one important respect, which is that however oddly they are put together, and making allowance for popularisation, both her science and her theology conform to thirteenth-century university teaching (*59*, pp.52-86, 88-111, 183-203; *60*, pp.203-78). Her confession isn't a thorough-going burlesque. Instead, as the continuation has worked 'up' the hierarchy of the philosophical dream vision, it has indeed gained a purchase on theological enlightenment; but it has done so by working 'down' a hierarchy of perception, since Nature is the principle of order in the material world, and has no part in the spiritual. In Nature, the two movements, upwards and downwards, meet in an uneasy and unstable way, but they *do* meet. And this is a tremendous challenge to traditional intellectual hierarchies: it seems momentarily possible that the material could be a guide to the spiritual, as indeed a woman's body comprehended the Trinity; and if so, what meaning can hierarchical categories such as 'material' and 'spiritual' continue to possess? What happens to traditional theories of knowledge? By raising such questions, the intellectual play in Nature's speech challenges traditional categories of language and perception.

(ii) Nature and gender

The unsettling of this material-spiritual hierarchy has an important corollary, in that medieval culture tended to discern a parallel between the relationship of mind to body and that of male to female. The figures of Adam and Eve, for example, were often read with Adam standing for the mind and Eve for sensuality. A somewhat softened version of this same equation is commonplace in courtly literature. We have already established its influence on GdL's *Rose*, in which the male lover is characterised by Amor and interacts with Raison, whereas the female love object is associated with Venus's torch. The view that women are dominated by the senses is expressed in JdM's continuation by Ami:

> Si sont eles voir presque toutes
> de prendre convoiteuses, et gloutes
> de ravir et de devorer,
> tant qu'il n'i puist rienz demorer
> a ceus qui plus por lor se claiment
> et qui plus loiaument les aiment;
> car Juvenaus si nous raconte
> qui de Berine tient son conte,
> que miex vosist un des yex perdre
> que soi a un seul homme aerdre,
> car nulz seus n'i peuïst soffire
> tant estoit de chaude matire. *   (8281-92 [8251-62])

Woman is an accumulation of physical appetites, insatiable sexual desire being the key to the others, the least excusable, most

---

* 'And truly they are almost all eager to take what they can, and greedy to snatch up and devour, so that they leave destitute those who most claim to be theirs and love them most loyally; for Juvenal relates in the story of Hiberina [*Satires* VI] that she would rather lose one of her eyes than cling to one man, for no man on his own can satisfy her, she was made of such hot matter.'

threatening, and best explained in terms of physiological difference (the 'heat' of 'matter'). Although Ami politely pretends that the lover's lady is an exception, his 'explanations' imply that virtuous women are not only rare, they are 'unnatural'. As the Vilain Jalous he invokes will say, such women are rarer than the phoenix or a white crow (8687-96 [8657-66]); only when a woman somehow receives a man's education, as Heloise did, can she be redeemed for rationality (8825-30 [8795-8800]).

Women are identified with the material in a further, important sense. Ami claims that neither he nor Solomon met a good woman, 'one who was *ferme*' (9924 [9894]). Genius later makes the same point:

> Que ja fame n'iert tant estable
> qu'el ne soit diverse et muable.* (16327-28 [16297-98])

Such instability aligns women with the material world of nature in general; for in her confession, Nature often refers to the contrast between the permanent or changeless, which is the domain of the supernatural, and her own, impermanent and subject to corruption:

> Je ne fis onc riens pardurables;
> quant que je fais est corrumpable.
> [...]
> Mi fait, ce dit, sont tuit soluble,
> tant ai pooir povre et onuble
> au regart de la grant poissance
> du Dieu qui voit en sa presence
> la triple temporalité
> sous un moment d'eternité. **
>   (19061-62, 19071-76 [19031-32, 19041-46])

---

* 'For woman can never be sufficiently stable as to prevent her from being various and changeable.'

** 'I never made anything eternal; everything I make is subject to corruption. [...] My deeds, [Plato] says, can all be dissolved, so poor and obscure is my power in comparison with the great might of God who can see before Him all three phases of time [past, present and future] in a single moment of eternity.'

In the *Rose* Nature and woman are analogues of each other, in a way which anthropologists have found to be common in many cultures (*57*). It is not surprising that Nature's female characteristics are repeatedly stressed in her confession. Yet as we have seen, Nature's speech challenges the hierarchical ranking of natural and supernatural, material and spiritual. If the easy hierarchy of mind over matter is undermined in JdM's *Rose*, where does this leave the male-female one?

I think that, as with the philosophical material, instability is introduced into the text by means of a clash between competing systems. The strident antifeminism launched by Ami and confirmed by the Vilain Jalous reaches its peak in Genius's 'comfort' of the weeping Nature. On the other hand the *Rose* gives a progressively greater voice to women and/or the feminine. After Ami the Vielle speaks; then Nature, who represents herself as a woman rather more than does Raison; finally, after a brief intervention by Genius, the dénouement is handed over to Venus. (For consideration of the problematic role of female figures of authority in the *Rose* and the philosophical tradition in which it stands, see *43*.) Rather than intersecting at a distinct point, however, the different valuations of gender co-exist throughout, and undermine each other.

The Vielle's speech, for example, gradually undermines misogynistic topoi. Initially she plays into the hands of antifeminism, claiming that she will use arguments from experience to prove that women should take as many lovers as they can and extract as much money from them as possible. She plans to train Bel Acuel, and use him to exact revenge from men for the wrongs they did to her. Her teaching centres on appearance and social behaviour: men can only be attracted and retained by women's looks, a fact so obvious Bel Acuel doesn't even need to be taught it (13079-92 [13049-62]). So where, we might ask, does sensuality lie? In women? Or in men? You need many lovers, continues the Vielle, because men are fickle:

Car il ont trop les cuers muables.
Jone genz ne sont pas estables. *   (13141-42 [13111-12])

This is the vocabulary of materiality/femininity, applied here to
men. Later in her 'lecture', the Vieille will cite examples of women
deserted by men – Dido, Medea – and stress the rarity of male
fidelity. The vocabulary of misogyny, familiar from Ami and the
Vilain Jalous, is here directed back at men.

Similar reversals are found in Genius's 'comfort' of Nature.
Women, he claims, will coax men's secrets out of them, and then
betray them with their uncontrollable talk (16347-68 [16317-38]).
However, as Genius's own narrative suggests, it is in fact the men
who cannot keep a watch on their tongues, since having resolved
not to tell their wives they all find themselves unable to keep silent
(16487-98 [16457-68]). The hierarchy opposing men's 'stability'
and 'constancy' to women's 'fickle garrulity' is dismantled.
Furthermore, the means whereby women extort these confidences,
according to Genius, is by exploiting their intimacy with their
husbands – like the duchess in the *Chastelaine de Vergi*, they
implicitly barter knowledge for sex:

Et sa fame vers li le tire.
qui bien voit qu'il est a mesaise,
si l'aplanie, acole et baise,
et le couche entre ses mameles:
'Sire,' dist elle, 'quex noveles?
Qui vous fait ensi soupirer
et tressaillir et revirer?' **   (16398-404 [16368-74])

If men can be identified with the mind, and women with the body,
as traditional thought would have it, this scenario shows how
temporary and provisional that identification is: for here women

---

* 'For their hearts are too changeable. Young men aren't reliable.'

** 'And his wife pulls [her husband] towards her, seeing his discomfort,
and strokes him, hugs and kisses him, and lays him between her breasts:
"Husband," she says, "what's up? Who is making you sigh and shiver and
toss about in this manner?"'

gain information and men gain physical gratification. Women, like JdM's Nature, come to possess knowledge which conventional hierarchies deny them (cf. *43*). And sexual gratification is the one thing which Genius urges men never to give up. They should flee women, he says (six times), but not to the extent that they don't sleep with them (16582-83, 16617-21 [16552-53, 16587-91])!

The gender hierarchy, like the mind-body hierarchy, is thus put in question. The traditional meanings assigned to 'maleness' and 'femaleness' are shown not to be grounded in biological difference. Instead, the reader of the *Rose* is made increasingly aware that the gender hierarchy is a political construct. The Vielle's speech is stylistically a parody of a university lecture (and thus, in the medieval context, of a discourse appropriate only to men), whilst its content derives mainly from Ovid, so we should not make the mistake of assuming that what she expresses is in any straightforward way a 'woman's point of view'. The lecture does, however, gradually 'explain' the faults traditionally attributed to women as the product of their political and economic disadvantages. If women exploit their looks, it is because they have no other forms of power. Men have money, mobility and the ability to take initiatives. Women's only exchangeable asset is their appearance. They are always at a position of disadvantage. Genius's 'comfort' of Nature confirms that the gender hierarchy is a product of politics, not biology. Knowledge must at all cost be withheld from women, because it puts men in their power (16641-44 [16611-14]). Hierarchies are not just intellectual. They are also political.

(iii) Nature and culture

It is not suprising to find a continuity, in JdM, between intellectual and political hierarchies; after all, writers like Abelard or Guillaume de Saint Amour who challenged traditional systems of thought were subject to censorship and punishment. The relation between mind and body is a political issue, if your body can be punished for the way you think.

The relation of male to female in JdM leads into analysis of political relations generally. In the rehearsals of the Golden Age myth by Ami and the Vielle, women figure as the archetypal form of property; and property is a fundamental social mechanism for the distribution and maintainance of power. Thus antifeminism is associated with a will to power, which is at its most apparent in the speech by the Vilain Jalous. He regrets that when you marry a woman you don't get the same opportunity to inspect the goods as you would when buying a horse (8667-77 [8637-47]). Although he regards all women as whores (9155-56 [9125-26]), he is upset by his wife's frigidity with him ('so that I get quite afraid', 9100 [9070]) – his own failure to 'possess' her makes him fear other men's success. He is particularly dismayed that others have the benefit of her fine clothes which to him are an unwanted expense (9254-70 [9234-40]). However, if a woman finds someone other than her husband to pay for her clothes, that is worse... The Jalous's misogyny rationalises his disappointment that a wife is not amenable to the same control as other forms of property.

The Vielle is no enthusiast for marriage, which she regards as oppressive of women's natural freedom. Ideally, men should be in common to all women and vice versa. Yet in the Vielle's view marriage places a necessary brake on men's rapacity; for before it, men simply seized the woman they wanted and then, when they tired of her, left her (13907-12 [13877-82]). Marriage is thus essentially a safeguard against rape. This is an implicit rebuke to Ami, who jauntily exhorts the dreamer to seize the rose with the old line that it's what women really want:

> Cuelliés la rose tout a force
> et moustrés que vous estes hons,
> quant lieus est et temps et sesons,
> car riens ne lor porroit tant plere
> comme tel force, qui la set fere. *   (7690-94 [7660-64])

Rape is also at issue in the story of Lucretia, related by the Vilain Jalous, but altered in such a way from its source as ironically to

---

* 'Take the rose by force and show that you're a man, when time and opportunity present themselves; nothing pleases [women] as much as that kind of force, if you know how to exercise it.'

undercut the speaker's determination to govern his own wife's body against her will. (For a study of this *exemplum* and that of Heloise, see *16*.)

The text therefore views the frustrations of marriage from two opposing points of view, in an argument which, as the Vielle's speech makes explicit, is about the values of nature and culture (see 13875-81 [13845-51], quoted above, and 13936-14160 [13906-14130]). Each sex looks to culture to remedy the fault in the 'nature' of the other sex: the Vilain Jalous deplores the way his wife retains what the Vielle will call her 'natural' liberty, and resists assimilation to other, more controllable, forms of property; the Vielle looks to the cultural institution of marriage to curb men's violence against women, whilst still allowing women a theoretical ('natural') right to sexual freedom.

Nature's speech makes an important contribution to this argument about hierarchy and power. The use of the Golden Age theme by all the other major speakers has familiarised the reader with the idea of a primal communism, where nature was abundant and there was no property, government or crime. Nature does, indeed, declare herself against reliance of any kind on material possessions. Her praise of clerks begins with an attack on a social hierarchy grounded in possessions, which, she agrees with Raison, are merely contingent on the whim of Fortune. She also opposes government by a hereditary caste, thus classing rank as a possession which is not 'natural'. For instance, she says that the body of a prince is worth no more than that of a carter, clerk, or cobbler (18592-93 [18562-63]). Her egalitarianism is founded in the identity of all men at birth:

> Par moi naiscent semblable et nu,
> fort et foible, gros et menu.
> Touz les met en equalité
> quant a l'estat d'umanité;
> Fortune y met le remanant,
> qui ne set estre permanent. * (18597-18602 [18567-72])

---

* 'Through me they are all, strong and weak, big and small, born alike and

Nature, then, seems to be putting her weight behind a social order that privileges the 'natural' over the 'cultural'. And yet this hierarchy is as unstable as the others we have seen. For one thing, it is clear that the kind of social hierarchy which Nature in fact promotes is based not on the body (as for example a blood aristocracy would be) but on the mind. For Nature, the 'noblest' members of society are those with virtue and intellect; such people will often be clerks, an order open to all levels of society (*61*, p.182), whom Nature praises at length. Thus, just as a physical and material Nature can provide knowledge of spiritual truths, so here, apparently, she provides the rationale for an intellectual meritocracy. Once again, the body-mind hierarchy is being played upon in a paradoxical way. Moreover, Nature is induced to lend support to Amor who, as the leader of a baronial army, surely embodies the kind of aristocratic social order which she reprobates. Finally, we should consider Amor's aims, and those of the lover. Amor is helping the lover towards sexual consummation, but has no thought at all for reproduction, which is Nature's primary purpose. To develop this point we need to return to GdL's text, and its relationship to JdM's continuation.

(iv) Nature, culture and GdL's 'Rose'

If intellectual play is more in evidence in JdM than in GdL's *Rose*, this is mainly because the continuation relies on exaggeration. It throws into relief the play with value-systems so characteristic of courtly texts. Though less boldly than in JdM, in GdL hierarchies are also placed in play. I have already commented on the mind-body paradox in GdL, whereby a garden of sensory delights is equivalent to a paradise garden; and on his presentation of gender, whereby the feminine is simultaneously exalted over the masculine and subsumed to it, represented simultaneously as powerful and as a speechless object. To these examples of paradox others can be added: (1) that of public and private: a public 'courtly' discourse is

---

naked; I make them all equal as regards their human status; Fortune gives them rest, which can only be impermanent.'

elaborated, the point of which, apparently, is to prevent anyone but true lovers from understanding it; (2) that of the licit and the transgressive: 'courtly' love is normative, indeed compulsory for the truly elegant, and yet sufficiently transgressive for lovers' dealings to be covered in secrecy. GdL's *Rose* plays with both of these oppositions. The teasing allegory inhibits access to meaning, so that confessional, autobiographical, and petitionary aspects of the poem are constantly mystified. The setting in what looks like a court, coupled with Amor's commands on the social responsibilities of the lover, suggest that love can take its place only within society; and yet the constant barriers placed between the lover and the object of his desire show that society is always on the defensive against lovers like him.

The play between the normative and the transgressive in GdL is enhanced because the representation of society in his text reflects historical hierarchies. In his part of the *Rose*, as in the world outside it, the rich rank higher than the poor, the leisured higher than the laborious, the aristocrat higher than the peasant. The aristocracy is in this period almost exclusively defined by inheritance: you are noble if your father and mother were noble. As the work of the social historian Georges Duby has shown, the aristocracy in the later twelfth century is strongly committed to regulating marriage and reproduction in order to safeguard the transmission of this inherited 'nobility' (*27*, pp.7-11). Yet to enter the garden of privilege in the *Rose*, and so qualify as a member of this wealthy, leisured and aristocratic milieu, one must become a lover. Amor, Deduit, his circle of couples, and eventually the lover himself, celebrate 'love' as a personal diversion, and act as though reproduction simply didn't exist. The garden of Deduit is thus paradoxical in so far as it reflects a courtly world predicated on birth, but promotes an ideal of heterosexual love from which reproduction is absent. In fact such love represents the greatest possible threat to a social hierarchy dependent on the strict regulation of reproduction and inheritance, but the 'peasant' Dangier is one of few figures in the garden to appreciate this! Thus from the point of view of 'courtliness', Deduit and Amor represent an 'order' threatened by Dangier and Jalousie, but from the point of view of aristocratic interest Dangier and Jalousie uphold an order to which Deduit and Amor are the threat.

I commented in Chapter 3 on the lyric qualities of GdL's text, its lack of forward impetus, and the dreamlike recurrence of the sense of frustration at encountering ever new obstacles. Those same observations bring home the anti-historical character of the first part of the *Rose*. In GdL Nature is placed, as it were, in opposition to history. The rose is a creature of nature; it is not to be removed from its natural setting; and in a wider sense, the lover, framed by the 'natural' setting of the garden, experiences love as part of a 'human nature', whose traits the various personifications enact. But this conception of love as an aspect of human nature is in conflict with the view of history which that same view of human nature implies – a history conceived as lineage, estates, and the devolution of 'nobility' and property over the generations.

In JdM Nature comes to the aid of the dreamer in the hope that, however little this may be his intention, he will impregnate the rose. And this indeed is what happens. The seeds mingle; the rose begins to swell (21727-30 [21697-21700]). The fiction which divorces love from reproduction is discarded at last; Jalousie and the uncourtly guardians of the rose are quite decisively routed, but aristocratic interests have suffered in the véry act of victory.

(v) *Nature, dreams and the problem of allegory*

The unsettling of hierarchies of ideas throughout the *Rose* takes place in the context of a dream, and dreams, in medieval thought, are also classified hierarchically. Macrobius, to whom GdL alludes in his prologue, uses a five-fold ranking in which the two lowest rungs are occupied by *insomnium* ('nightmare') and *visum* ('apparition, sexual fantasy') (cf. *24*, p.575). GdL's prologue insists that dreams contain veiled truths, and thereby repudiates these 'lower' dreams in favour of the higher kind: *somnium* ('enigmatic dream'), *visio* ('prophetic dream'), and *oraculum* ('oracular dream'). These higher dreams, which are susceptible of more than one level of reading, are 'allegorical', as we saw in Chapter 2.

Dreams, then, resemble the imagination, whose range of functions extends from sensory delusion to spiritual revelation (cf. Chapter 5, pp.89-91). The 'lower' dreams belong with the physical end of the scale, and the 'higher' ones with its spiritual potentialities. Since Nature stands at a crossroads in the text between an 'upwards' spiritualising movement, and a 'downwards' sexualising one, her opinion of dreams is especially significant. And her position turns out to be uncompromising: dreams, she says, are empty delusions. Two points of contact with GdL's prologue, the rhyme *songe : mençonge*, and an allusion to the dream of Scipio on which Macrobius's work is a commentary, emphasise that her words are a rebuttal of the prologue's claims:

> et ce n'est fors trufle et mençonge,
> ausinc cum de l'omme qui songe,
> qui voit, ce cuide, en lor presences
> les espirituex sustances
> si cum fist Scipion jadis. * (18363-67 [18333-37])

What is the reader to make of the poem in the light of this contradiction?

As with the other issues discussed in this chapter, GdL's part of the *Rose* already admits paradox. Although his prologue may claim to inaugurate spiritual truths, the general drift of his text appears to celebrate worldly love, and to fall altogether into the category of sensual delusion, where indeed the subsequent developments of Nature's speech will place it (see 18383ff. [18353ff.], and Chapter 2, pp.16-18). Conversely, much of Nature's discourse points to exactly the kind of theological matter that an enigmatic dream might be supposed to yield. These ironies have been resolved in different ways by previous critics. Dahlberg, for example, maintains that GdL's text is actually a denunciation of sexual love, and so recuperates 'spiritual' truth from it (*24*, p.576 ff.). I think, however, that once again Nature is involved in the

---

* '...and all it is is trifles and lies, as it is for the man who dreams and sees, or so he imagines, spiritual essences in their actuality, like Scipio did of old.'

disturbance of a hierarchy related to that between mind and body, spirit and flesh. Her words assert that the *somnium* is, from a 'natural' point of view, only a *visum*; that is, that a spiritual vision is only a sensual delusion. Far from helping us to understand what 'physical' and 'spiritual' might mean, her words make the issue of knowledge and understanding more elusive than it was before.

This time, it is the form of the text that is at stake, as well as its content. For if a *somnium* is, 'naturally' a *visum*, then the distinction between letter and spirit, which is a final variant of the body-soul hierarchy, is also in trouble (cf. *56*, pp.56-63, and above, p.89). Over all these disruptive moves Nature smiles, a figure of the 'natural', the most elusive term of all.

JdM's continuation has often been seen as a triumph of 'naturalism'. It is true that the idea of nature dominates his text, just as Nature's speech is its high point, its most glorious poetic passage. But this is not to say that there is a consistent view of the 'natural' or of the 'naturalistic' to be found in the *Rose*. On the contrary, Nature is the most mobile figure in JdM's intellectual play. While she represents the coherence of the material universe, she also dispenses theology. While she is identified with a misogynistic presentation of the feminine, she also helps to undermine antifeminism. While she represents the necessity of bodily reproduction, she denies that any 'nobility' is transmitted by birth, since authority belongs, not in her realm of the material, but in the domain of Raison. Nature, it seems, is a vital term in the construction of any hierarchy, intellectual or political; any value system we propose will be defended on the grounds that it is 'natural', and the fact that such systems conflict with one another does not prevent us from invoking her. It is 'natural' for the planets to revolve and 'natural' for man to exercise free will to resist their influence; 'natural' for women to be subordinate and 'natural' that they should seek to gratify their desires; 'natural' for us to reproduce ourselves but 'unnatural' to think that we can thereby reproduce a valid political system. The conflicting uses of the term 'nature' show us more about our thought processes, than about the constitution of the world.

In all the intellectual hierarchies considered in this chapter, it is the lower term of the pair which, although seemingly inferior, apparently triumphs over its higher-placed partner. The material encroaches on the spiritual as the feminine on the masculine, the delusory on the visionary and the literal on the allegorical. Nature is party to all this disruption; for if it is 'natural' to believe contradictory propositions, Nature is also that which frustrates and dwarfs human efforts at imposing order. If we think of the world as orderly and neatly ranked, so that we imagine that we control it, that is largely an effect of language, an effect that 'nature', with its astonishing mobility, can quickly overturn.

In Nature and her disruptiveness, JdM confronts the opacities of our beliefs, the incoherence of the intellectual discourses that deal with them, and the folly of deluding ourselves that linguistic order or system corresponds to any real control over reality. The elegant paradoxes of courtly rhetoric, which maintain (among other things) that it is 'natural' to desire what would undermine a 'natural' aristocracy, and 'natural' to ignore the possibility of reproduction in a society based on birth, provide him with a perfect starting point for this comic *tour de force*. The dream which might have some profound message to dispense, but might equally turn out to be an erotic fantasy, is its perfect medium.

7. Beyond A Joke

The ending of the *Romance of the Rose* is a foregone conclusion, announced by Amor at the mid point of the completed text (10599 ff. [10569 ff.]), anticipated by several other personifications (e.g. the Vielle, 12753 [12723]), and actively schemed for by most of them. It is made the more inevitable by its provocative deferral; indeed, the prolonged deliberations of the personified abstractions, many of whom have cosmic powers, give the *Rose* something of the quality of a shaggy-dog story: a basically simple joke, expanded out of all proportion by elaborate digressions that both stave off, and offset, a trivial punch-line.

Although the poem's ending relieves the fear that the text will turn out, after all, to be interminable, it cannot be said to be a resolution. As I have shown, the *Rose* combines two quests, the erotic and the philosophical. The erotic quest ends when the lover gets the rose, but the quest for enlightenment remains unfulfilled. What is it, after all, that the lover has 'got', and what have we learned from his getting it?

Amor himself had pointed out that the difficulties ahead lay not in finishing the text but in expounding it. With Guillaume de Lorris none too bright, and Jean de Meun not yet born, this problem seems insuperable:

> Puis vodra si la chose espondre
> que rienz ne s'i porra repondre.
> Se cil conseil metre i peüssent,
> tantost consillié m'en eüssent;
> mes par cesti ne puet or estre,
> ne par celi qui est a nestre,
> car il n'est mie ci presens.
> Et la chose rest si pesans
> que certes, quant il sera nés,

se je n'i vienz touz empenés
por lire li nostre sentence
si tost cum il istra d'enfence,
ce vouz os jurer et plevir
qu'il n'en porroit jamés chevir. *
　　　　　　　　(10603-16 [10573-86])

This unresolved quest for enlightenment has continued almost without interruption since the thirteenth century. The turn of the fourteenth and fifteenth century witnessed the famous literary *querelle* which pitted Christine de Pizan and Jean Gerson (who denounced the *Rose* as scurrilous and impious) against various humanist defenders of Jean de Meun – principally Pierre and Gontier Col, and Jean de Montrueil. (The documents in this debate have been edited and presented in *10*; see also *15*, pp.411-89.) In the early sixteenth century, the *Rose* was reworked by Jean Molinet, who sought to eliminate 'undesirable' features and make it more unequivocally pious (*74*, pp.237-84); it was also revised by Marot (*55*). Later it was admired by Ronsard and Du Bellay as the only product of the Middle Ages worth preserving. Badel has compiled a list of references to it from 1429 to 1640 (*15*, pp.507-11) which attest to its enduring readability. When the Enlightenment began to turn a scholarly eye towards the Middle Ages, the *Rose* was the first medieval text to be edited (in 1745); it has since been the object of successive re-editions and a vast body of critical writing, of which the items in the bibliography to this study are only a sample. The *Rose* quest also continued in the works of other poets. The fourteenth century saw numerous literary responses to the *Rose*, which have been discussed by Badel (*15*, pp.73-409). JdM can

---

* 'Then he [JdM] will wish to explicate the matter in such a way as to leave nothing hidden. If they [GdL and JdM] could advise me on this, they would have done so. But this one here [GdL] can't do it now, nor can the other who is still to be born, because he simply isn't here. And furthermore the matter is so weighty that indeed, even when he is born, I can swear and promise you he will never be able to manage it unless I come to him with my feathered wings to read him our judgement, as soon as he has left childhood behind.'

include Machaut. Villon. Chaucer and Dante among his most distinguished readers and commentators (see *14*, pp.68-86). In all these enterprises. the meaning and nature of the text are at stake.

The *Rose* is not an easy poem to like in the twentieth century. Much of its material is drawn from sources unfamiliar to the modern reader. Yet its preoccupations – sexuality, society, knowledge and language – are those of many writers widely admired today. such as Freud. Lacan or Foucault; I think there are considerable similarities between JdM and Derrida (*25*, cf. *44*, pp.83-84). The poem's elusive and ironic manner, and allegorical framework, can make it appear abstruse. They also, however, make it infinitely rewarding. Whatever intellectual inquiry one brings to the *Rose*, whatever critical position one seeks to test, the text seems already to have anticipated it. to be there before one, smiling at the reader's efforts. That smile is hard to judge. Alive with intelligence, both sardonic and benign. it is inscrutably seductive.

The narrator recounts a dream in which he walks along a river until reaching a walled garden (1-133). On the outside of the wall are depicted Haïne, Felonie, Vilenie, Convoitise, Avarice, Envie, Tristesse, Vielece, Papelardie and Pauvreté (134-460 [134-462]). He gains admission through a narrow gate guarded by Oiseuse, and witnesses a round dance led by Deduit and including Courtoisie, Amor, Biauté, Richece, Verité, Largece, Franchise and Leesce (461-1300 [463-1298]). After a while he wanders off, unaware that Amor is following him. He reaches a rose garden, which is reflected in the waters of a spring identified by an inscription as where Narcissus died (1301-1614 [1299-1612]). The dreamer looks into the water and singles out one particular rosebud. Amor fires five arrows at him: Biauté, Simplece, Franchise, Compaignie and Biau Semblant (1615-1880 [1613-1878]). He then accepts homage from the dreamer and tells him the commandments of love, and what it is like to be a lover; the dreamer is told he can call on the help of Douz Regart, Douz Parler, Douz Penser and Esperance. Then Amor disappears (1881-2778 [1879-2762]). The dreamer approaches the rose, encouraged by Bel Acuel, but when he tries to touch it he is driven off by Dangier, Malebouche, Honte and Poor (2779-970 [2763-954]). Raison descends from her tower and tries to dissuade him from allegiance to Amor, but he rejects her (2971-3106 [2955-3080]). Ami appears, and advises the dreamer to mollify Dangier with the help of Franchise and Pitié. He approaches Bel Acuel again, and this time asks for a kiss which, thanks to Venus, he gets (3107-498 [3081-480]). However Malebouche has told Jalousie of these events, and she builds a castle around the rose garden, placing guards at its four corners, and appointing the Vielle to keep a watch on Bel Acuel (3499-980 [3481-952]). The narrator stands lamenting outside the walls of Jalousie's castle (3981-4058 [3953-4028]).

[From this point, the text is taken over by Jean de Meun.] Despondent, the dreamer begins to regret not having listened to Raison (3953-4220 [4029-190]). She reappears and tells him to abandon earthly loves except 'good love' and to regard sexual love merely as a means to reproduction. The dreamer should love only Raison herself. The dreamer rejects this advice, and reaffirms his allegiance to Amor (4221-7230 [4191-7200]). Ami then reappears, and offers prolific advice on seduction. In the course of his speech, the luckless role of a jealous husband is presented in monologue form by the Vilain Jalous. Ami concludes by recommending a short cut to success: the Chemin de Trop Doner (7231-10002 [7201-9972]). The Lover reflects that Ami is wiser than Raison and goes in search of Richece, but she chases him away (10003-267 [9973-10237]). The dreamer then encounters Amor, renounces Richece, and rehearses the ten commands of love. Amor praises Jean de Meun to his court of barons and asks for their advice in combatting Jalousie. A plan is formed whereby the the castle guards will be murdered and the Vielle bribed to assist the lover (10268-918 [10238-888]). Fausemblant introduces himself, together with his companion Contrainte Abstinence. Together they murder Malebouche (10919-12380 [10889-12350]). Courtoisie and Largece then win the Vielle's support, and she proceeds to lecture Bel Acuel on the best way to handle men. Bel Acuel rejects the worldlier parts of her advice (12381-14678 [12351-14648]). The Vielle brings the dreamer to attempt to pluck the rose, but Dangier chases him away once more, supported by Honte and Poor, and Bel Acuel is imprisoned again (14679-15044 [14549-15014]). In response to the dreamer's cries for help, Amor's army goes into action. Venus comes to their aid and all swear a solemn oath to combat Chastaé (15045-890 [14015-15860]). Nature at her forge hears the oath, which comforts her in her grief at a 'sin' she has committed, and which she confesses to her priest Genius. All the world obeys her, except for man who is recalcitrant in perpetuating the species as he should. She repents having made him and sends Genius to Amor's army to bless and encourage them in their efforts (15891-19438

[15861-19408]). Genius preaches a sermon anathematising all who fail to make proper use of the sexual organs given them by Nature. Only thus will they achieve salvation. He criticises Guillaume de Lorris for praising the garden of Narcissus rather than the park of the Lamb (19439-20669 [19409-20639]). With the help of Amor's army and Venus's torch, the castle is successfully stormed, the dreamer gets the rose, and the dream comes to an end (20670-21780 [20640-21750]).

Bibliography

ROMANCE OF THE ROSE

(i) editions

1. *Le Roman de la Rose*, ed. Ernest Langlois, 5 vols (Paris: Firmin-Didot, S.A.T.F., 1914-24)
2. *Le Roman de la Rose*, ed. Felix Lecoy, 3 vols (Paris: Champion, coll. C.F.M.A., 1965-70)
3. *Le Roman de la Rose*, ed. Daniel Poirion (Paris: Garnier Flammarion, 1974)

(ii) translations

4. · *The Romance of the Rose by Guillaume de Lorris and Jean de Meun*, translated by Charles Dahlberg (Princeton: Princeton UP, 1971; 3rd edn, 1995)
5. *The Romance of the Rose*, translated by Frances Horgan (Oxford: OUP, World's Classics, 1994)

OTHER MEDIEVAL TEXTS

6. Adam de la Halle, *The Chansons of Adam de la Halle*, edited with introduction, notes and glossary by J.H. Marshall (Manchester: MUP, 1971)
7. Alan of Lille, *Anticlaudianus or the Good and Perfect Man*, translation and commentary by James J. Sheridan (Toronto: Pontifical Institute of Medieval Studies, 1973)
8. ——, *The Plaint of Nature*, translation and commentary by James J. Sheridan (Toronto: Pontifical Institute of Medieval Studies, 1980)
9. Boethius, *The Consolation of Philosophy*, translated with an introduction by V.E. Watts (Harmondsworth: Penguin, 1969)
10. Hicks, Eric, *Le Débat sur le Roman de la Rose* (Paris: Champion, 1977)
11. Jean de Meun, 'Boethius's *De consolatione* by Jean de Meun', ed. V.L. Dedeck-Héry, *Medieval Studies*, 14 (1952), 165-275.
12. ——, *Li lettere di Abelardo ed Eloisa nella traduzione di Jean de Meun*, ed. Fabrizio Beggiato, 2 vols (Modena: STEM-Mucchi, 1977)

13. Schroth, R., *Eine altfranzösische Übersetzung des Consolatio Philosophiae des Boethius (Handschrift Troyes Nr. 898)*. *Edition und Kommentar* (Berne: Herbert Lang; Frankfurt/M.: Peter Lang, 1976)

MODERN STUDIES

(A skeletal bibliography, including introductory works, is indicated by asterisks)

*14. Arden, Heather M., *The Romance of the Rose* (Boston: Twayne, Twayne's World Authors Series, 1987)

15. Badel, Pierre-Yves, *Le Roman de la Rose au XIVe siècle: étude de la réception de l'oeuvre* (Geneva: Droz, Publications romanes et françaises, 1980)

16. Baumgartner, Emmanuèle, 'De Lucrèce à Héloïse, remarques sur deux exemples du *Roman de la Rose* de Jean de Meun', *Romania*, 95 (1974), 433-42

17. Bloch, R. Howard, *The Scandal of the Fabliaux* (Chicago: University of Chicago Press, 1986)

18. ——, 'Medieval Misogyny', *Representations*, 20 (1987), 1-24

19. Brook, Leslie C., 'The Translator and his Reader: Jean de Meun and the Abelard-Heloise Correspondence', in *The Medieval Translator* II, ed. Roger Ellis (London: Westfield Publications in Medieval Studies 5, 1991), pp.99-122

20. Brownlee, Kevin, 'Jean de Meun and the Limits of Romance. Genius as Rewriter of Guillaume de Lorris', in *Romance. Generic Transformations from Chrétien de Troyes to Cervantes*, ed. Kevin Brownlee and Marina Scordilis Brownlee (Hanover and London: University Press of New England, 1985), pp.114-34

21. Calin, William, *A Muse for Heroes. Nine Centuries of the Epic in France* (Toronto: Toronto UP, 1983)

22. Cerquiglini, Jacqueline, 'Le Clerc et l'écriture: le *Voir Dit* de Guillaume de Machaut et la définition du dit', in *Grundriss der romanischen Literaturen des Mittelalters. Literatur in der Gesellschaft des Spätmittelalters*, ed. Hans Ulrich Gumbrecht (Heidelberg: Winter, 1980), pp.151-68

23. Chenu, Marie-Dominique, *La Théologie au douzième siècle* (Paris: Vrin, 1957)

24. Dahlberg, Charles, 'Macrobius and the Unity of the *Roman de la Rose*', *Studies in Philology*, 58 (1961), 573-82

25. Derrida, Jacques, *La Dissémination* (Paris: Seuil, 1972)

26. Dragonetti, R., 'Pygmalion ou les pièges de la fiction', in *Orbis medievalis. Mélanges... R.R. Bezzola* (Berne: Francke, 1978), pp.89-111

27. Duby, Georges, *Medieval Marriage. Two Models from Twelfth-century France* (Baltimore and London: Johns Hopkins UP, 1978)

28. Fleming, John V., *The 'Roman de la Rose': A Study in Allegory and Iconography* (Princeton: Princeton UP, 1969)

29. ——, *Reason and the Lover* (Princeton: Princeton UP, 1984)

30. Friedman, Lionel J., '"Jean de Meung", Antifeminism, and "Bourgeois Realism"', *Modern Philology*, 57 (1959-60), 13-23

31. Gunn, Alan M.F., *The Mirror of Love. A Reinterpretation of the 'Romance of the Rose'* (Lubbock, Texas: Texas UP, 1952)

32. Helsinger, Howard, 'Pearls in the Swill: Comic Allegory in the French Fabliaux', in *The Humor of the Fabliaux*, ed. Thomas D. Cooke and Benjamin L. Honeycutt (Columbia, Missouri: University of Missouri Press, 1974), pp.93-105

33. Hill, Thomas D., 'La Vieille's Digression on Free Love: A Note on Rhetorical Structure in the *Romance of the Rose*', *Romance Notes*, 8 (1966-67), 113-15

*34. ——, 'Narcissus, Pygmalion and the Castration of Saturn: Two Mythographic Themes in the *Roman de la Rose*', *Studies in Philology*, 71 (1974), 404-26

35. Huchet, Jean-Charles, *Littérature et psychanalyse. Pour une clinique littéraire* (Paris: PUF, 1990)

*36. Hult, David F., *Self-fulfilling Prophecies. Readership and authority in the first 'Roman de la Rose'* (Cambridge: CUP, 1986)

*37. Huot, Sylvia, *From Song to Book. The Poetics of Writing in Old French Lyric and Narrative Poetry* (Ithaca and London: Cornell UP, 1987)

38. ——, *The Romance of the Rose and its Medieval Readers: Interpretation, Reception, Manuscript Transmission* (Cambridge: CUP, 1993)

*39. Jauss, Hans Robert, 'La Transformation de la forme allégorique entre 1180 et 1240: d'Alain de Lille à Guillaume de Lorris', in *L'Humanisme médiéval dans les littératures romanes du XIIe au XIVe siècle*, ed. A. Fourrier (Paris: Klincksieck, 1964), pp.107-44

40. Jung, Marc-René, *Etudes sur le poème allégorique en France* (Berne: Francke, 1971)

41. Kay, Sarah, *Subjectivity in Troubadour Poetry* (Cambridge: CUP, 1990)

42. ——, 'The Birth of Venus in the *Romance of the Rose*', in a special volume of *Exemplaria*, ed. Kevin Brownlee, 1996 (forthcoming)

43. ——, 'Women's Body of Knowledge in the *Romance of the Rose*', in *Framing Medieval Bodies*, ed. Sarah Kay and Miri Rubin (Manchester: MUP, 1994), pp.211-35

44. ——, 'Sexual Knowledge: the Once and Future Texts of the *Romance of the Rose*', in *Textuality and Sexuality*, ed. Judith Still and Michael Worton (Manchester: MUP, 1993), pp.69-86

45. Kelly, Douglas, *Medieval Imagination. Rhetoric and the Poetry of Courtly Love* (Madison: University of Wisconsin Press, 1978)

46. Kuhn, Alfred, 'Die Illustration des *Rosenromans*', *Jahrbuch der Kunsthistorischen Sammlungen der allerhöchsten Kaiserhauses*, 31 (1913-14), 1-66

47. Langlois, Ernest, *Les Manuscrits du Roman de la Rose. Description et classement* (Paris: Champion; Lille: Tallandier, 1910)

48. Lewis, C.S., *The Allegory of Love* (Oxford: OUP, 1936)

49. Louis, René, *Le Roman de la Rose. Essai d'interprétation de l'allégorisme érotique* (Paris: Champion, 1974)

50. Mann, Jill, *Geoffrey Chaucer* (New York etc.: Harvester-Wheatsheaf, 1991)

51. Michaud-Quantin, Pierre, 'La Classification des puissances de l'âme au XIIe siècle', *Revue du Moyen Age Latin*, 5 (1949), 15-34

52. Milan, Paul B., 'The Golden Age and the Political Theory of Jean de Meun', *Symposium*, 23 (1969), 137-49

53. Murray, Alexander, *Reason and Society in the Middle Ages* (Oxford: Clarendon Press, 1978)

54. Muscatine, Charles, 'The Emergence of a Psychological Allegory in Old French Romance', *Publications of the Modern Language Association of America*, 68 (1953), 1160-83

55. Nichols, Stephen G., Jr., 'Marot, Villon and the *Roman de la Rose*', *Studies in Philology*, 64 (1967), 25-43

56. Nitzsche, Jane Chance, *The Genius Figure in Antiquity and the Middle Ages* (New York and London: Columbia UP, 1975)

57. Ortner, Sherry B., 'Is Female to Male as Nature is to Culture?', in *Woman, Culture and Society*, ed. M. Rosáldo and L. Lamphere (Stanford: Stanford UP, 1974), pp.67-88

58. Ott, Karl August, 'Jean de Meun und Boethius', *Philologische Studien. Gedenkschrift für Richard Kienast*, ed. Ute Schwab and Elfriede Stutz (Heidelberg: Winter, 1978), pp.193-227

59. Paré, Gérard, *Le 'Roman de la Rose' et la scolastique courtoise* (Paris and Ottawa: Publications de l'Institut d'Etudes Médiévales d'Ottawa, 1941)

60. ——, *Les Idées et les lettres au XIIIe siècle. Le 'Roman de la Rose'* (Montréal: Publications de l'Institut d'Etudes Médiévales Albert-le-Grand, 1947)

61. Payen, Jean Charles, *La Rose et l'Utopie* (Paris: Editions Sociales, 1976)

62. Payen, Jean Charles, 'Le Comique de l'énormité: goliardisme et provocation dans le *Roman de la Rose*', *L'Esprit Créateur*, 16 (1976), 46-60

63. ——, '*Le Roman de la Rose* et la notion de carrefour idéologique', *Romanistische Zeitschrift für Literaturgeschichte*, 1 (1977), 193-203

64. Pelen, Marc M., *Latin Poetic Irony in the 'Roman de la Rose'* (Liverpool: Cairns, 1987)

*65. Poirion, Daniel, 'Narcisse et Pygmalion dans le *Roman de la Rose*', in *Essays in Honour of Louis Francis Solano* (Chapel Hill: University of North Carolina Press, 1970), pp.153-165

*66. ——, *Le Roman de la Rose* (Paris: Hatier, 1973)

67. ——, 'Les Mots et les choses selon Jean de Meun', *Information Littéraire*, 26 (1974), 7-11.

*68. Polak, Lucie, 'Plato, Nature and Jean de Meun', *Reading Medieval Studies*, 3 (1977), 80-103

69. Robertson, D.W., Jr., 'The Doctrine of Charity in Medieval Literary Gardens: a Topical Approach through Symbolism and Allegory', *Speculum*, 26 (1951), 24-49.

70. Smith, Nathaniel B., 'In Search of the Ideal Landscape: From *Locus amoenus* to *Parc du Champ Joli* in the *Roman de la Rose*', *Viator*, 11 (1980), 225-43

71. Stock, Brian, *The Implications of Literacy. Written Language and Models of Interpretation in the Eleventh and Twelfth Centuries* (Princeton: Princeton UP, 1983)

*72. Strubel, Armand, *Le Roman de la Rose* (Paris: PUF, 1984)

73. Topsfield, Leslie, 'The *Roman de la Rose* of Guillaume de Lorris and the Love Lyric of the Early Troubadours', *Reading Medieval Studies*, 1 (1975), 30-54

74. Tuve, Rosemond, *Allegorical Imagery. Some Medieval Books and their Posterity* (Princeton: Princeton UP, 1966)

75. Uitti, Karl D., 'From Clerc to Poète: the Relevance of the Romance of the Rose to Machaut's World', in *Machaut's World. Science and Art in the Fourteenth Century*, ed. Madeleine Pelner Cosman and Bruce Chandler (New York: Annals of the New York Academy of Sciences, 314, 1978), pp.209-216.

76. Vitz, Evelyn Birge, 'The *I* of the *Roman de la Rose*', *Genre*, 6 (1973), 49-73

77. Wetherbee, Winthrop, 'The Literal and the Allegorical: Jean de Meun and the *de Planctu Naturae*', *Medieval Studies*, 33 (1971), 264-91

78. ——, *Platonism and Poetry in the Twelfth Century. The Literary Influence of the School of Chartres* (Princeton: Princeton UP, 1972)

79. ——, 'The Theme of Imagination in Medieval Poetry and the Allegorical Figure of Genius', *Mędievalia et Humanistica*, 7 (1976), 45-64
80. Zink, Michel, *La Subjectivité littéraire* (Paris: PUF, 1985)
81. Zumthor, Paul, 'Narrative and Anti-Narrative: Le *Roman de la Rose*', in *Approaches to Medieval Romance*, Yale French Studies, 51 (1974), 185-204

Since I wrote this book, a new edition has appeared: *Le Roman de la Rose*, ed. Armand Strubel (Paris: Livre de Poche, série Lettres gothiques, 1992). It contains the text with a facing translation in modern French. Its line numbers are up to 4 lines ahead of those in the editions by Poirion and Langlois, and thus up to 34 lines ahead of those in the Foulet edition. Unfortunately, Strubel's base manuscript lacks the last folio, and the end of the poem is presented in translation only. There have also been a number of further critical works, the most important of which are Susan Stakel, *False Roses. Structures of Duality and Deceit in Jean de Meun's 'Roman de la rose'* (Stanford French and Italian Studies, 69, Stanford: Anma Libri, 1991) and a collection of essays, *Rethinking the 'Romance of the Rose'.Text, Image, Reception,* edited by Kevin Brownlee and Sylvia Huot (Philadelphia: University of Pennsylvania Press, 1992).

CRITICAL GUIDES TO FRENCH TEXTS

edited by
Roger Little, Wolfgang van Emden, David Williams